T0255701

GameMaker: Studio 100 Programming Challenges

Ben Tyers

Apress®

GameMaker: Studio 100 Programming Challenges

Ben Tyers
Worthing, West Sussex, United Kingdom

ISBN-13 (pbk): 978-1-4842-2643-8 ISBN-13 (electronic): 978-1-4842-2644-5
DOI 10.1007/978-1-4842-2644-5

Library of Congress Control Number: 2017932374

Managing Director: Welmoed Spahr
Lead Editor: Steve Anglin
Development Editor: Matthew Moodie
Technical Reviewer: Dickson Law
Coordinating Editor: Mark Powers
Copy Editor: Karen Jameson
Compositor: SPi Global
Indexer: SPi Global
Artist: SPi Global
Cover image designed by Freepik

Distributed to the book trade worldwide by Springer Science+Business Media New York, 233 Spring Street, 6th Floor, New York, NY 10013. Phone 1-800-SPRINGER, fax (201) 348-4505, e-mail orders-ny@springer-sbm.com, or visit www.springeronline.com. Apress Media, LLC is a California LLC and the sole member (owner) is Springer Science + Business Media Finance Inc (SSBM Finance Inc). SSBM Finance Inc is a Delaware corporation.

For information on translations, please e-mail rights@apress.com, or visit www.apress.com.

Apress and friends of ED books may be purchased in bulk for academic, corporate, or promotional use. eBook versions and licenses are also available for most titles. For more information, reference our Special Bulk Sales–eBook Licensing web page at www.apress.com/bulk-sales.

Any source code or other supplementary materials referenced by the author in this text are available to readers at www.apress.com/9781484226438. For detailed information about how to locate your book's source code, go to www.apress.com/source-code/.

Printed on acid-free paper

Contents at a Glance

Contents

About the Author

Ben Tyers is a freelance programmer and technical writer by day and a sci-fi horror novel writer by night. He made his first computer game way back in 1984, on a ZX Spectrum 48K computer, when he was eight years old. His passion for creation has continued since then. He holds a number of computer-related qualifications. When relaxing, Ben has an infatuation for old-school horror and sci-fi films, particularly 1960s B-Movies.

About the Technical Reviewer

Dickson Law is a GameMaker hobbyist, commentator, and extension developer with six years of community experience. In his spare time, he enjoys writing general-purpose libraries, tools, and articles covering basic techniques for GameMaker Studio. As a web programmer by day, his main areas of interest include integration with server-side scripting and API design. He lives in Toronto, Canada.

Acknowledgments

Many Thanks to the Following:

Music:

David Szesztay Cheese
Scott Holmes Happy Go Lucky
Broke For Free Night Owl
Urbano A. Zafra Danza Filipina

ghost sprite: @XenosNS
Shadow Script: Peter Christian Jørgensen
Board Game Sprites: Kenney.nl
Fire Particle Effect & Sprites: Martin Crownover - `http://martincrownover.com`
Destructible Terrain: roychanmeliaz
Croc Image: iconarchive.com
Random Terrain: Reed Hector
Dartboard: VectorPortal.com
Dart: `http://www.gifmania.co.uk/`
Blood Splatter: PWL - OpenGameArt.org
Bullet Sprites: Master484 - `http://m484games.ucoz.com/`
Zombie Sprites: Riley Gombart / ChessMasterRile - OpenGameArt.org
Tower Defence Sprites: nido
Colour Palette<a href='`http://www.freepik.com/free-vector/color-palette-background_758007.htm`'> Designed by Freepik</a>
GMLscripts.com - see: GMLscripts.com/license. For the Following Scripts:
dec_to_bin dec_to_hex dec_to_oct dec_to_roman
draw_get_button motion_predict
Chess Sprites: mr0.0nerd : `https://2dartforgames.wordpress.com/`
Parallax backgrounds: Pasilan

Big Thanks to:
Vadim
"YellowAfterlife"
Dyachenko

—Doug Morrison

Introduction

This book contains 100 programming challenges to test your prowess as a programmer in GameMaker: Studio's GML.

You do not have to start this book at the beginning; just delve in and select a challenge for the time you have available.

The task that needs to be completed is stated for each challenge. Each challenge has a difficulty rating, and is worth a set number of points. A level 1 challenge is worth 10 points; a level 2 is worth 20 points; up to level 5, which is worth 50 points. An estimated time to complete the challenge is stated, whether you gauge yourself as a beginner of GML, have a medium skill level, or consider yourself advanced. You only get points if you complete it within the allotted time.

In addition to the task page, each has a guide that provides some of the more important GML required for solving the task. You may use GameMaker: Studio's Help File (by pressing F1), which will not lose you any points. You may not search on the Internet.

Each task has an additional challenge, each of which carries 20 points. There is no time limit for this additional challenge.

There is a marking table at the back of the book that allows you to take note of your progress.

Each main challenge has a downloadable GMZ project file showing an example solution. There may be more than one way to solve a challenge.

All resources can be accessed by clicking the Download Source Code button at `www.apress.com/9781484226438`.

CHALLENGE 1

Maths Bar Graph

Challenge Outline

To accept 5 fieldnames / legends and numerical inputs (a value between 1 and 100), for each input.
Display a bar graph showing each value graphically with the corresponding fieldname / legend under each.

Level 2

Beginner 3 Hours
Medium 1 Hour
Advanced 30 Minutes

Additional Challenge

Create an onscreen keyboard to allow appropriate data to be entered. Limit fieldname to between 1 and 20 characters, and check integer value is between 1 and 100. Allow user to specify colour of each bar graph element.

Points

In Time 20
Additional 20

Notes on Approaching This Challenge

For this you will need to figure out how to input text and variables in and how to draw text and rectangles using these inputs. A suitable method for storing the inputs would be a 2-dimensional array.

Electronic supplementary material The online version of this chapter (doi:10.1007/978-1-4842-2644-5_1) contains supplementary material, which is available to authorized users.

B. Tyers, *GameMaker: Studio 100 Programming Challenges*, DOI 10.1007/978-1-4842-2644-5_1

Guide

You can input data in using:

```
text=get_string("name","");
```

or

```
value=get_integer("integer",0);
```

You can draw a rectangle:

```
draw_rectangle(10,10,50,50,true);
```

where the values are `x1,y1,x2,y2,outline`
and the last value can be true or false for drawing outline or not.

You can format text, for example, the alignment, font style, and colour:

```
draw_set_halign(fa_center);
draw_set_font(font_text);
draw_set_colour(c_blue);
```

Note, that when you set drawing styles - including text alignment, font and colour - they will apply to all future drawings unless set otherwise.

You can repeat a block of code:

```
repeat(10)
{
//repeats 10 times
}
```

CHALLENGE 2

Draggable and Movable Object

Challenge Outline

Create an object with a sprite set. Allow instances of this object to be dragged using the left mouse button.

Level 1

Beginner 45 Minutes
Medium 30 Minutes
Advanced 12 Minutes

Additional Challenge

Create multiple instances. When releasing moved instance over another instance, place above it. If attempting to move from a location where multiple instances are present, only select and move the uppermost one.

Points

In Time 10
Additional 20

Notes on Approaching This Challenge

For this challenge you will need to check if the mouse cursor is over an instance. You can do this by checking the ID under the mouse position.

You will also need to compensate for the object's sprite origin.

B. Tyers, *GameMaker: Studio 100 Programming Challenges*, DOI 10.1007/978-1-4842-2644-5_2

Guide

You can check whether the mouse is over an instance using:

```
if position_meeting(mouse_x,mouse_y,id)
{
//do something
}
```

You can check for the initial mouse press using:

```
if mouse_check_button_pressed(mb_left)
{
//do something
}
```

You can check for continued pressing of a button:

```
if mouse_check_button(mb_left)
{
//do something
}
```

You can update the instance's position to the mouse coordinates:

```
x=mouse_x;
y=mouse_y;
```

CHALLENGE 3

Room Fade In and Out Transition

Challenge Outline

Create a system that fades a room to solid black, goes to a new room, and then fades from black to fully transparent.

Level 1

Beginner 25 Minutes
Medium 15 Minutes
Advanced 8 Minutes

Additional Challenge

Allow the option of setting the fade colour and speed.
Add 2 additional fade effects:
Scroll in from Side
Fade between Rooms

Points

In Time 10
Additional 20

Notes on Approaching This Challenge

You'll need to figure out how to draw a solid rectangle and set its alpha that changes over a number of steps.

B. Tyers, *GameMaker: Studio 100 Programming Challenges*, DOI 10.1007/978-1-4842-2644-5_3

Guide

You can set alpha for drawing functions using:

```
draw_set_alpha(value);
```

Where `value` is a value between 0 (transparent) and 1 (opaque)
For example:

```
draw_set_alpha(0.5);
```

Would set the transparency at 50%.

■ **Note** Apply alpha applies to all future drawing functions until set otherwise. You should set back to 1 when you're done so as not to affect unrelated drawing routines.

You can increase a value gradually each step, for example, by placing this in a Step Event:

```
value+=0.1;
```

This would increase by 0.1 per step.
You can decrease a value gradually each step, for example:

```
value-=0.1;
```

This would decrease by 0.1 per step.
You can draw a rectangle:

```
draw_rectangle(10,10,50,50,true);
```

where the values are `x1,y1,x2,y2,true/false`
Where last value can be `true` or `false.` `True` will only draw an outline; `false` will draw as a solid.
You can check if a value has exceeded another value:

```
if valuea>valueb
{
//do something
}
```

CHALLENGE 4

Typewriter Text Effect

Challenge Outline

To display a string one character at a time. Make a keyboard click sound as each new letter is shown.

Level 2

Beginner 45 minutes

Medium 30 Minutes

Advanced 8 Minutes

Additional Challenge

Allow bold and italic formatting and choice of text colour.

Points

In Time 20

Additional 20

Notes on Approaching This Challenge

For this task you'll need to figure out how to get a character from a string at a given position.

A good method for this is to take a character and add to a new string.

Use an alarm to allow a pause between characters being drawn. An audio file for the click sound is included in the resources pack.

B. Tyers, *GameMaker: Studio 100 Programming Challenges*, DOI 10.1007/978-1-4842-2644-5_4

Guide

You can set text to a string variable:

```
example="hello # world";
```

forces a line break

You can retrieve a single character at a position from a string:

```
string_char_at(text_to_write, i);
```

You can return the number of characters in a string:

```
length=string_length(example);
```

Playing audio is pretty straightforward:

```
audio_play_sound(snd_example,1,false);
```

CHALLENGE 5

Audio Volume Change Based on Distance

Challenge Outline

To change the volume of a music track depending on how far the player is from another object: the farther away, the lower the volume.

Level 2

Beginner 30 Minutes
Medium 20 Minutes
Advanced 8 Minutes

Additional Challenge

Create the same effect using audio emitters.
Create four music tracks, each playing in a corner of the room.
Make the falloff point at the room's center.

Points

In Time 20
Additional 20

Notes on Approaching This Challenge

There a few ways to approach this. You could use the functions audio_play_sound_at and audio_listener_position. Alternatively you could use audio_emitter_* functions. For this task we will use audio_play_sound_at and audio_listener_position for its simplicity.

B. Tyers, *GameMaker: Studio 100 Programming Challenges*, DOI 10.1007/978-1-4842-2644-5_5

Guide

You can use:

```
audio_play_sound_at(soundis,x,y,z,falloff_dist,falloff_max_dist,
falloff_factor,loop,priority);
```

to play a sound at the given location.

You can create a listener using:

```
audio_listener_position(x, y, z);
```

Note that an improper up value (z) would reverse the channels.

For more advanced use, you can look at using `audio_listener_orientation`, which can be used to adjust the audio depending on the direction of the listener.

CHALLENGE 6

Move Object to Position Using Path

Challenge Outline

When the mouse right button is pressed, create a path that moves the player to a new position while avoiding obstacles.

Level 2

Beginner 1 Hour
Medium 30 Minutes
Advanced 8 Minutes

Additional Challenge

Cause the object to rotate to the path direction before moving. Then ensure the object is always pointing in direction it is moving.

Points

In Time 20
Additional 20

Notes on Approaching This Challenge

For this task you'll need to know basic `mp_grid_*` and `path_*` functions.

B. Tyers, *GameMaker: Studio 100 Programming Challenges*, DOI 10.1007/978-1-4842-2644-5_6

Guide

You can create a mp_grid using:

```
size=16;//set grid size
grid = mp_grid_create(0,0,ceil(room_width/size),ceil(room_height/size),size,size);
//create mpgrid;
```

You can add instances to avoid using:

```
mp_grid_add_instances(grid,obj_obstacle,1);
```

It's possible to overwrite with a new path:

```
mp_grid_path(grid,path,x,y,target_x,target_y,true);
```

You can create a path:

```
path=path_add();
```

And start an instance on a path:

```
path_start(path, 2, path_action_stop, true);
```

You should ensure that the path is not constantly set every step or won't move at all.

You can delete a path using `path_delete()`. You should do this at the Room End and destroy the instance if it is not persistent.

CHALLENGE 7

Make the Screen Shake

Challenge Outline

Make the room shake when S is pressed.

Level 2

Beginner 30 Minutes
Medium 15 Minutes
Advanced 6 Minutes

Additional Challenge

Make objects and backgrounds shake independently.

Points

In Time 20
Additional 20

Notes on Approaching This Challenge

The easiest way to approach this is by using views.

B. Tyers, *GameMaker: Studio 100 Programming Challenges*, DOI 10.1007/978-1-4842-2644-5_7

Guide

You can change a view using:

```
view_xview[0]=value;
view_yview[0]=value;
```

where value can be a positive or negative number.

You can check for a key being held down:

```
if keyboard_check(ord('S'))
{
//do something
}
```

And key being released:

```
if keyboard_check_released(ord('S'))
{
//do something
}
```

You can create a random number within a range. For example:

```
value=irandom_range(-10, 10);
```

which would create a whole random number between -10 and 10.

■ **Note** Using non-integer values may create interpolation issues, especially on a scaled view.

CHALLENGE 8

Create Snow Effect

Challenge Outline

Create a falling snow effect with two different sizes of snowflakes.

Level 1

Beginner 20 Minutes
Medium 12 Minutes
Advanced 3 Minutes

Additional Challenge

Create the effect using a particle system. Have different sized snowflakes that move at different speeds.

Points

In Time 10
Advanced 20

Notes on Approaching This Challenge

You can use the built-in effects system for this.

B. Tyers, *GameMaker: Studio 100 Programming Challenges*, DOI 10.1007/978-1-4842-2644-5_8

Guide

You can create an effect using:

```
effect_create_above(type, x,y,size,colour);
```

where type can be:

`ef_cloud`, `ef_ellipse`, `ef_explosion`, `ef_fireword`, `ef_flare`, `ef_rain`, `ef_ring`, `ef_smoke`, `ef_smokeup`, `ef_snow`, `ef_spark`, and `ef_star`.

For `ef_rain` and `ef_snow`, x and y coordinates do not matter.

CHALLENGE 9

Password Easter Egg

Challenge Outline

Allow user to enter a password using the keyboard. Do not use get_string. Make the password bacon. Allow the pressing of X to clear any password entered.

Level 2

Beginner 40 Minutes

Medium 20 Minutes

Advanced 10 Minutes

Additional Challenge

Reduce the player's score by 100 if player pressed x and then enters the wrong password.

Points

In Time 20

Additional 20

Notes on Approaching This Challenge

You'll need to figure out which variable stores recently pressed keyboard letters. Also figure out how to reset this if x is pressed.

B. Tyers, *GameMaker: Studio 100 Programming Challenges*, DOI 10.1007/978-1-4842-2644-5_9

Guide

You can check for a certain keypress using:

```
if (keyboard_check_pressed(ord('X')))
{
//do something
}
```

Recent keys pressed are held in this variable:

```
keyboard_string
```

that can be reset using:

```
keyboard_string= "";
```

You can test a string variable against another string

```
if string== "hello"
{
//do something
}
```

CHALLENGE 10

Follow Two Objects in View

Challenge Outline

Create two player objects, one movable by arrow keys, the other by WSAD.
Put this in a large (4000x4000) room.
Create a control object that keeps both players' objects in view by changing the view.

Level 2

Beginner 1 Hours
Medium 40 Minutes
Advanced 30 Minutes

Additional Challenge

Create a similar system that works with three objects.

Points

In Time 20
Additional 20

Notes on Approaching This Challenge

For this you'll need to use room views, view, and view port settings.

B. Tyers, *GameMaker: Studio 100 Programming Challenges*, DOI 10.1007/978-1-4842-2644-5_10

Guide

Simple movement can be done by detecting keypresses, for example:

```
if (keyboard_check(ord('A')))  {x-=5;}
```

or

```
if (keyboard_check(vk_left))  {x-=5;}
```

You can get the x and y position of the first instance of an object, for example:

```
xposition = obj_player1.x;
```

You can set a view width by using:

```
view_wview[0]=value;
```

and a height:

```
view_hview[0]=value;
```

It's possible to set the x position of view with:

```
view_xview[0]=value;
```

Similarly for the y position:

```
view_yview[0]=value;
```

also you can return the value of the current view port:

```
width=view_wport[0];
height=view_hport[0];
```

CHALLENGE 11

High / Low Number Game

Challenge Outline

Computer picks a random number between 1 and 100.
Player guesses by entering a number.
The computer tells you if the number is too high or too low.
Player keeps guessing until the number is found.

Level 1

Beginner 1 Hour
Medium 25 Minutes
Advanced 11 Minutes

Additional Challenge

Create a GUI interface to allow player to enter guesses.

Points

In Time 10
Additional 20

Notes on Approaching This Challenge

First you'll need to create a random number for the player to guess - and then a method of allowing the player to enter their guess. You'll then require some conditionals to check the guess against the random number.

B. Tyers, *GameMaker: Studio 100 Programming Challenges*, DOI 10.1007/978-1-4842-2644-5_11

Guide

You can get a random integer using, for example:

```
value=irandom_range(1,50);
```

You can see if a guess is higher than another value:

```
if guess>value
{
//do something
}
```

Likewise, you can see if a guess is lower than another value:

```
if guess<value
{
//do something
}
```

or equal using:

```
if guess==value
{
//do something
}
```

One method of getting input from a player is:

```
guess=get_integer("Your Guess", 0);
```

CHALLENGE 12

Calculate the Average Position of Two Clicks

Challenge Outline

Allow player to click twice in the room using the mouse, storing the x and y position of each click.
Place an X at the average location.

Level 1

Beginner 30 Minutes
Medium 20 Minutes
Advanced 8 Minutes

Additional Challenge

Allow for up to 10 clicks, again finding the average position of all clicks.

Points

In Time 10
Additional 20

Notes on Approaching This Challenge

You'll need store the locations of the mouse clicks and then perform the necessary math to find the average position. Then place an object at that position.

B. Tyers, *GameMaker: Studio 100 Programming Challenges*, DOI 10.1007/978-1-4842-2644-5_12

Guide

You can store the X position of the mouse:

```
xpos=mouse_x;
```

similarly for the y position.

You can place an instance of an object:

```
instance_create(x,y,object);
```

You can set a variable:

```
variablename=value;
```

where value is a number.

You can increment a variable by 1 using:

```
variablename++;
```

You can check a variable's value, for example:

```
if variablename ==1
{
        //do something
}
```

CHALLENGE 13

■ ■ ■

Retrieve Text File from Web and Save Locally

Challenge Outline

To retrieve a text file from a website, save locally, and then display the contents onscreen.

Level 2

Beginner 1 Hour

Medium 40 Minutes

Advanced 20 Minutes

Additional Challenge

Combine this with challenge 80 to retrieve level design that you've uploaded.

Points

In Time 20

Additional 20

Notes on Approaching This Challenge

For this task you'll need to use an asynchronous event, basic file handling, an array, and text drawing.

B. Tyers, *GameMaker: Studio 100 Programming Challenges*, DOI 10.1007/978-1-4842-2644-5_13

Guide

You can start the file retrieval using:

```
file = http_get_file("http://gamemakersbook.com/test.txt",working_directory +"test.txt");
```

Asynchronous code must be placed in the relevant asynchronous event.
If you don't have Internet access you can add test.txt as an included file, and skip this step.
In this challenge it may look like:

```
if ds_map_find_value(async_load, "id") == file//sets up map
    {
    var status = ds_map_find_value(async_load, "status");//gets status
    if status == 0//status 0 means file is finished downloading
       {
       //probably not best to run every step, just here as an example
    file=file_text_open_read(working_directory +"test.txt");//open file for reading
    while (!file_text_eof(file))//loops until end of file
    {
        str[num++] = file_text_readln(file);//reads a line and adds to array
    }
    file_text_close(file);//closes file
    read=true;.
      }
    }
```

CHALLENGE 14

Shuffle Pack of Playing Cards and Deal 5

Challenge Outline

Take 52 playing card sprites, shuffle them, and then deal out the top 5 cards when D is pressed.

Level 3

Beginner 1 Hour
Medium 40 Minutes
Advanced 20 Minutes

Additional Challenge

Deal out 3 hands of 5 cards. Determine which hand is the best poker hand.

Points

In Time 30
Additional 20

Notes on Approaching This Challenge

Ds_lists will be your friend here. They allow you to add, shuffle, and remove contents. You will also require a few loops of some kind.

B. Tyers, *GameMaker: Studio 100 Programming Challenges*, DOI 10.1007/978-1-4842-2644-5_14

Guide

You can create a new ds list with:

```
list_name=ds_list_create();
```

You can add a single element to a list:

```
ds_list_add(list_name, value);
```

You can also add multiple elements at the same time:

```
ds_list_add(list_name, value1, value2, value3);
```

where value can be variables, sprite names, objects, etc.

If a list contains more than one element, you can shuffle the order:

```
ds_list_shuffle(list_name);
```

It's also possible to use an accessor to return a value at a position, for example:

```
value=list_name[|2];
```

which would return the value at position 2. Note: the first position in a ds list is 0.

You can also delete at a position:

```
ds_list_delete(list_name,0);
```

which would cause other elements in the list to shift up one position.

CHALLENGE 15

Reverse Sentence Order

Challenge Outline

Create a sentence. Take this sentence and reverse the word order.

Level 3

Beginner 1 Hour
Medium 40 Minutes
Advanced 20 Minutes

Additional Challenge

Keep the word order, but reverse all letters.

Points

In Time 30
Additional 20

Notes on Approaching This Challenge

One approach is to take a letter at a time until you get a [space] then add this word to a suitable data structure. Repeat this until all words are found or until you reach the end of the sentence.

Guide

You can get a single letter from a string.

```
letter = string_copy(sentence, position, 1);
```


B. Tyers, *GameMaker: Studio 100 Programming Challenges*, DOI 10.1007/978-1-4842-2644-5_15

You can add strings together:

```
new_string=string1+string2;
```

You can get the length of a string:

```
no_of_characters=string_length(sentence);
```

You can add a string to an array's cell:

```
array[position]=value;
```

also you can decrement a value in a for loop:

```
for(loop = 10; loop >-1 ; loop -= 1)
{
}
```

which would count from 10 down to 0;

CHALLENGE 16

Rotate and Move Object to Mouse Position

Challenge Outline

To make an object rotate so it points toward the mouse, then slowly moves to the mouse position.

Level 1

Beginner 40 Minutes
Medium 20 Minutes
Advanced 8 Minutes

Additional Challenge

Rotate to point to mouse via shortest rotation angle. Only start moving when pointing at mouse +/- 10 degrees.

Points

In Time 10
Additional 20

Notes on Approaching This Challenge

A function exists for calculating the direction between 2 objects. You can use this value to set the direction and image angle of an object.

B. Tyers, *GameMaker: Studio 100 Programming Challenges*, DOI 10.1007/978-1-4842-2644-5_16

Guide

You can get the angle from one position to another:

```
angle=point_direction(x,y,x2,y2);
```

You can set what direction an instance moves in:

```
direction=angle;
```

You can also rotate an instance's sprite to face a direction:

```
image_angle=angle;
```

and set the speed an instance moves at:

```
speed=2;
```

CHALLENGE 17

Firework Display Using Effects

Challenge Outline

To create a fireworks display using the effects that GM provides.

Level 1

Beginner 20 Minutes
Medium 10 Minutes
Advanced 5 Minutes

Additional Challenge

Create a fireworks display using the particle system.

Points

In Time 10
Additional 20

Notes on Approaching This Challenge

GameMaker has a basic built-in effects system. You can use this to create some impressive effects.

Guide

You can create a firework effect at a given position, size, and colour, for example.

```
effect_create_above(ef_firework,x,y,1,c_green);
```


B. Tyers, *GameMaker: Studio 100 Programming Challenges*, DOI 10.1007/978-1-4842-2644-5_17

You can get a random position in the room's width with:

```
xposition=random(room_width);
```

and the room's height:

```
yposition=random(room_height);
```

You can choose one from a set at random:

```
random_colour=choose(c_red,c_green,c_blue);
```

CHALLENGE 18

Random Sentence Generator

Challenge Outline

To create random sentences when S is pressed and display on screen. The sentences should (to a point) make sense.

Level 5

Beginner 1 Hour
Medium 30 Minutes
Advanced 15 Minutes

Additional Challenge

Display the text as a side scrolling marquee effect.

Points

In Time 50
Additional 20

Notes on Approaching This Challenge

For each part of the sentence you'll need to choose from a selection of options. This could be achieved using a ds list, array, or choose function.

B. Tyers, *GameMaker: Studio 100 Programming Challenges*, DOI 10.1007/978-1-4842-2644-5_18

Guide

Using a ds_list approach:

You can create a ds list and add to it:

```
name=ds_list_create();
ds_list_add(name, "Ben","Steve","Joe");
```

then shuffle it:

```
ds_list_shuffle(name);
```

and get a value:

```
selection=name[| 0];
```

Using an array approach:

```
name[0]= "Ben";
name[1]= "Steve";
name[2]= "Joe";
```

and get a value:

```
selection=name[irandom(3)];
```

You can add strings together:

```
sentence=name+place;
```

CHALLENGE 19

Pop-Up RPG Style Text Box

Challenge Outline

Create a system that allows you to queue messages and show them one at a time. Draw the messages as text, above a rectangle that only shows when a message does.

Level 4

Beginner 3 Hours
Medium 1 Hour
Advanced 30 Minutes

Additional Challenge

Allow the setting of drawing text colour.

Points

In Time 40
Additional 20

Notes on Approaching This Challenge

A ds list can be used to queue the messages. You can get the message at the top of the list and display this, removing it as you go.

B. Tyers, *GameMaker: Studio 100 Programming Challenges*, DOI 10.1007/978-1-4842-2644-5_19

Guide

You can create a ds list with:

```
global.list=ds_list_create();
```

You can add to a list:

```
ds_list_add(global.list, "example");
```

You can retrieve the top value (if it exists):

```
example=ds_list_find_value(global.list,0);
```

You can remove at a position, for example:

```
ds_list_delete(global.list,0);
```

You can get the size of a list:

```
size=ds_list_size(global.list);
```

CHALLENGE 20

Room Wrapping

Challenge Outline

To make an object wrap around the screen on all sides.
For example, if it goes off the left of the screen, it then appears on the right. Do the same for right, top, and bottom.

Level 1

Beginner 30 Minutes
Medium 10 Minutes
Advanced 6 Minutes

Additional Challenge

Compensate for a GUI Border of 50 pixels on top, left, and right, and a border of 150 at the bottom.

Points

In Time 10
Additional 20

Notes on Approaching This Challenge

For this you will need to use conditionals to test the x and y positions of the object and move to a new position as required. Having the sprite origin set as center will make this easier.

B. Tyers, *GameMaker: Studio 100 Programming Challenges*, DOI 10.1007/978-1-4842-2644-5_20

Guide

You can check the value of a current x position using:

```
if x==value {do something}
```

or you can check if x is greater than a value:

```
if x>value {do something}
```

You can move the x position for example:

```
x=value;
```

so the code may look like:

```
if x>100
{
x=1;
}
```

Simple code to move the player:

```
if (keyboard_check(ord('A')))  {x-=5;}
if (keyboard_check(ord('D')))  {x+=5;}
if (keyboard_check(ord('W')))  {y-=5;}
if (keyboard_check(ord('S')))  {y+=5;}
```

CHALLENGE 21

Sprite Shadow

Challenge Outline

Draw a shadow of a sprite, in a different colour than the original sprite.

Level 3

Beginner 1 Hour

Medium 30 Minutes

Advanced 12 Minutes

Additional Challenge

Create a Sun that moves across the screen. Make the shadow depending on the angle of the Sun.

Points

In Time 30

Additional 20

Notes on Approaching This Challenge

draw_sprite_ext will be your friend here. It will allow you to use more advanced drawing. Changing the sprite origin is also a useful method you may wish to investigate.

Guide

You'll only need one function for this, draw_sprite_ext.

```
draw_sprite_ext( sprite name, sub image, x, y, x scale, y scale, rotation, colour, alpha );
```


B. Tyers, *GameMaker: Studio 100 Programming Challenges*, DOI 10.1007/978-1-4842-2644-5_21

An explanation of the above variables:

`sprite name` is the name of your sprite, for example `spr_boat`.

sub-image is the sprite's sub-image, which can also be `0` or `image_index`.

x and y is where to draw, relative to the sprite's origin. You may wish to add / subtract here to give the appearance of an angle for the shadow, for example x-4, y-2.

x scale and y scale relate to the scale size; 1 is full size, 0.5 would be half size, 2 would be double.

`rotation` will rotate the image, for example, a value of 5 would rotate 5' anticlockwise.

`colour` is the colour blend; use c_black to shade black.

`alpha` is of course the transparency to draw at.

CHALLENGE 22

Make a Jukebox Player for Four Songs

Challenge Outline

To create a simple music player that plays 4 music tracks. Have a separate button for each track. When a button is clicked, stop any music already playing and play the selected track.

Level 1

Beginner 40 Minutes
Medium 20 Minutes
Advanced 8 Minutes

Additional Challenge

Display how much time is left when a track is playing.

Points

In Time 10
Additional 20

Notes on Approaching This Challenge

For this challenge you'll need to use basic audio handling. There are 4 tracks in the resources you can use for this challenge.

B. Tyers, *GameMaker: Studio 100 Programming Challenges*, DOI 10.1007/978-1-4842-2644-5_22

Guide

You can check if a track is playing and stop it:

```
if audio_is_playing(track1)
{
audio_stop_sound(track1);
}
```

You can start a track:

```
audio_play_sound(track1,1,false);
```

The final value determines whether the sound is looped, `true`, or plays just once, `false`.

You can check if the mouse is over a button using the following in a Step Event; alternatively just use Left Mouse Button Pressed Event:

```
if position_meeting(mouse_x,mouse_y,id) && mouse_check_button_pressed(mb_left)
{
        //do something
}
```

CHALLENGE 23

Scrolling Credits

Challenge Outline

Create a string that gives the credits of a game. Make the text scroll up from the bottom of the screen. Create it so that when the last credit has left the screen, the object is destroyed.

Level 2

Beginner 1 Hour
Medium 30 Minutes
Advanced 15 Minutes

Additional Challenge

Get the credits from a text file; one is provided in the resources.

Points

In Time 20
Additional 20

Notes on Approaching This Challenge

For this project you'll need a variable that holds the credits as a string. You can set the horizontal alignment to center and find out how many pixels high the credits are.

B. Tyers, *GameMaker: Studio 100 Programming Challenges*, DOI 10.1007/978-1-4842-2644-5_23

Guide

You can draw text at an x and y position onscreen, for example:

```
draw_text(50,50, "hello");
```

You can force a line break using #; for example:

```
text= "hello # world";
draw_text(50,50,text);
```

when drawn would put "hello" on the first line and "world" on the second line.

You can get the height in pixels; for example:

```
height=string_height(text);
```

You can change the y (vertical) position, for example:

```
y-=1;
```

You can also test the y position, for example:

```
if y==100
{
	//do something
}
```

CHALLENGE 24

Random Dice Roller

Challenge Outline

To randomly roll 5 dice and display the results graphically. Have a button to roll the dice.

Level 3

Beginner 1 Hour

Medium 30 Minutes

Advanced 12 Minutes

Additional Challenge

Roll 4 hands of 5 dice. Award a point to the highest hand(s).

Points

In Time 30

Additional 20

Notes on Approaching This Challenge

For this challenge you'll be good to use a separate sprite sub-image for each dice face. You can use `irandom` to choose a value. You'll also need a button object that can be pressed to choose random dice rolls. There are some dice sprites in the resources pack.

B. Tyers, *GameMaker: Studio 100 Programming Challenges*, DOI 10.1007/978-1-4842-2644-5_24

Guide

You can choose a random number within a range, for example:

```
number=irandom_range(1,10);
```

which would choose a random whole number between 1 and 10 inclusive.

You can draw a certain sub-image of a sprite:

```
draw_sprite(spr_name,sub_image,100,100);
```

You can detect a mouse button released with the following code in a Step Event; alternatively use the Right Mouse Button Released Event:

```
if position_meeting(mouse_x,mouse_y,id) && mouse_check_button_released(mb_right)
{
        //do something
}
```

CHALLENGE 25

Substitution Cipher

Challenge Outline

A substitution cipher is where each letter of the original text is replaced by a different letter.
Allow a user to enter a sentence. Apply a substitution cipher and display the result.

Level 2

Beginner 1 Hour
Medium 30 Minutes
Advanced 10 Minutes

Additional Challenge

Allow user to enter a cipher, then convert this back to the original text.

Points

In Time 20
Additional 20

Notes on Approaching This Challenge

For this you'll need some form of loop to go through each character of a message. You'll also need various string handling, like getting a character from a position, testing a character at a position, and adding strings together.

B. Tyers, *GameMaker: Studio 100 Programming Challenges*, DOI 10.1007/978-1-4842-2644-5_25

Guide

You can get a string in by using:

```
text= get_string("Enter Some Text:", "");
```

You can get the length in characters of a string:

```
characters= string_length(text);
```

You can get the character at a given position:

```
char = string_char_at(text, position);
```

You can find at what position a character is present:

```
pos = string_pos(char, text);
```

You can add strings together:

```
new_string=string1+string2;
```

You can repeat a block of code using a for loop, which would repeat for the value of loop from 1 to 19 inclusive:

```
for (var loop = 1; loop < 20; loop += 1)
{
        //do something
{
```

CHALLENGE 26

Save Highscore to INI

Challenge Outline

To create an INI system to save the highscore. Display the current highscore on screen. Create a button to allow the user to enter a new score, updating the INI file if the score is bigger. Show a message to indicate whether highscore has been updated or not.

Level 3

Beginner 40 Minutes
Medium 25 Minutes
Advanced 10 Minutes

Additional Challenge

Allow the user to enter their name to display next to the score. Display the best 3 scores.

Points

In Time 30
Additional 20

Notes on Approaching This Challenge

For this challenge you'll need basic integer handling and simple INI file functions.

B. Tyers, *GameMaker: Studio 100 Programming Challenges*, DOI 10.1007/978-1-4842-2644-5_26

Guide

You can check if a value is greater than another:

```
if value1>value2
{
        //do something if value1 is bigger
}
else
{
        //do something if it isn't
}
```

You can open an INI file:

```
ini_open("filename.ini");
```

You can read a real number from an INI file:

```
data=ini_read_real("section", "key", real_value);
```

You can write a real number to an INI file using:

```
ini_write_real("section", "key", real_value);
```

You can read a string from an INI file:

```
data=ini_read_string("section", "key", string_value);
```

You can write a string to an INI file using:

```
ini_write_string("section", "key", string_value);
```

You should close an INI file as soon as you are finished with it:

```
ini_close();
```

You can show a message:

```
show_message("This is a message");
```

CHALLENGE 27

Spawn Point

Challenge Outline

To create 4 spawn points. When a player object collides with it, the player remembers the position. If T is pressed, the player spawns back at last spawn point.

Level 2

Beginner 1 Hour
Medium 40 Minutes
Advanced 20 Minutes

Additional Challenge

Make the player return to the last spawn point by following a path between current position and the last spawn point, avoiding any objects.

Points

In Time 20
Additional 20

Notes on Approaching This Challenge

For this you'll need some basic movement code for the player, a way to detect a collision, and a way to store the x and y positions.

B. Tyers, *GameMaker: Studio 100 Programming Challenges*, DOI 10.1007/978-1-4842-2644-5_27

Guide

You can use the following for simple movement code:

```
if (keyboard_check(ord('A')))  {x-=5;}
if (keyboard_check(ord('D')))  {x+=5;}
if (keyboard_check(ord('W')))  {y-=5;}
if (keyboard_check(ord('S')))  {y+=5;}
```

You can test for a collision with another object:

```
if place_meeting(x,y,object_name)
{
        //do something
}
```

You can store the position:

```
x_position=x;
y=position=y;
```

You can move back to a stored position:

```
x=x_position;
y=y_position;
```

CHALLENGE 28

Dictionary Check

Challenge Outline

User enters a word, and the program checks if it exists within a dictionary text file. It then displays a message showing whether it exists or doesn't. A text file is present in the resources that you can use for this.

Level 3

Beginner 2 Hours
Medium 1 Hour
Advanced 30 Minutes

Additional Challenge

Create an onscreen keyboard to allow appropriate data to be entered.

Points

In Time 30
Additional 20

Notes on Approaching This Challenge

For this you'll need some basic file handling, and some data structure to store the words in.

B. Tyers, *GameMaker: Studio 100 Programming Challenges*, DOI 10.1007/978-1-4842-2644-5_28

Guide

You can open a text file with:

```
reference=file_text_open_read("file.txt");
```

You can retrieve each line from a text file with:

```
while(!file_text_eof(reference))
{
    line=file_text_read_string(reference);//store text in line
    file_text_readln(reference);//read to next line
}
```

You can create a ds list:

```
list_name=ds_list_create();
```

You can add to a ds list using:

```
ds_list_add(list_name,line);
```

You can check if a value exists in a ds list:

```
position = ds_list_find_index(dictionary, word_to_find);
```

which will return the position of where the reference is stored, if it is not present it will return -1.

CHALLENGE 29

Draw Text with Shadow

Challenge Outline

To draw text with a shadow.

Level 1

Beginner 25 Minutes
Medium 15 Minutes
Advanced 8 Minutes

Additional Challenge

Create a script that also allows you to set the font, text colour, and shadow colour.

Points

In Time 10
Additional 20

Notes on Approaching This Challenge

You'll need to draw the text twice, each with a separate colour and position.

B. Tyers, *GameMaker: Studio 100 Programming Challenges*, DOI 10.1007/978-1-4842-2644-5_29

Guide

You can set some text to a variable:

```
text="This is some random text to show a shadow of text.";
```

You can set a font (that has been created):

```
draw_set_font(font_example);
```

You can set a drawing colour:

```
draw_set_colour(c_blue);
```

You can draw text at a position:

```
draw_text(x_pos,y_pos,text);
```

CHALLENGE 30

Classic Brick and Ball Game Remake

Challenge Outline

Create a simple remake of the classic brick and ball game.
Have a player bat that can be controlled by the keyboard.
Have a brick that the player tries to hit with a ball.

Level 2

Beginner 1 Hour
Medium 40 Minutes
Advanced 20 Minutes

Additional Challenge

Create a highscore system based on the amount of time player took to complete the level

Points

In Time 20
Additional 20

Notes on Approaching This Challenge

You'll need simple keyboard input, collision detection, and movement for this.

B. Tyers, *GameMaker: Studio 100 Programming Challenges*, DOI 10.1007/978-1-4842-2644-5_30

Guide

Simple movement for player:

```
if (keyboard_check(vk_left))  {x-=5;}
if (keyboard_check(vk_right))  {x+=5;}
```

To start the ball moving:

```
motion_set(180,5);
```

which would set the ball moving left at a speed of 5. These values can be replaced by variables.

To make a ball bounce (in a collision event):

```
move_bounce_all(true);
```

CHALLENGE 31

Fire Projectile

Challenge Outline

To fire an object from a control object toward the mouse position.

Level 1

Beginner 1 Hour
Medium 40 Minutes
Advanced 30 Minutes

Additional Challenge

Base the speed of the object on how long the mouse button is held.

Points

In Time 10
Additional 20

Notes on Approaching This Challenge

You'll need to work out how to get the coordinates of a position and direct an object to that location and set the speed.

B. Tyers, *GameMaker: Studio 100 Programming Challenges*, DOI 10.1007/978-1-4842-2644-5_31

Guide

You can create an object and apply a reference to it:

```
reference=instance_create(x,y,object);
```

You can then access it change its attributes, for example:

```
reference.x=25;
```

which would change its x positon.

You can get the direction from one object to another:

```
dir=point_direction(x,y,target_x,target_y);
```

and use this to apply a direction, for example:

```
direction=dir;
```

The following variables hold the mouse's position:

```
mouse_x
mouse_y
```

The variable speed is speed in pixels. You can set this using, for example:

```
speed=5;
```

or based on a created reference:

```
reference.speed=5;
```

CHALLENGE 32

World Clock

Challenge Outline

Display the current time in 2 major cities (one ahead of your local time and one behind), as well as your local time. Display hours and minutes as texts. If an element has a single digit, pad it out with a leading 0, or 00 for between midnight and 1 a.m.

Level 4

Beginner 1 Hour
Medium 40 Minutes
Advanced 20 Minutes

Additional Challenge

Also display the time in a separate analog clock for each time.

Points

In Time 40
Additional 20

Notes on Approaching This Challenge

GameMaker has built-in variables that hold the current time, minutes, and hours - you may look these up in the help file.

B. Tyers, *GameMaker: Studio 100 Programming Challenges*, DOI 10.1007/978-1-4842-2644-5_32

Guide

You can set the program to use UTC time (known in the UK as GMT).

```
date_set_timezone(timezone_utc);
```

Or set according the clock time on your PC:

```
date_set_timezone(timezone_local);
```

You can get the local hour time from your pc using:

```
london_hour=date_get_hour(date_current_datetime());
```

and similarly for minutes and seconds.

If you're adding or subtracting from your local hour you may end up with a value below 0 or above 24. You can correct this: for example, if you wanted to take 6 hours off you would add 18 (24-6) and then apply mod 24:

```
value=(value+18) mod 24;
```

You can convert an integer to a string, for example:

```
str=string(value);
```

You can get the length of a string:

```
length=string_length(str);
```

You can test the length of a string:

```
if length==5
{
        //do somthing
}
```

You can combine two or more strings/string variables together:

```
new="hello"+str;
```

CHALLENGE 33

Text-Based Quiz

Challenge Outline

Store questions and answers in a text file, with 3 options for each question and an additional value to flag the correct answer.
Display the question, answer options, and correct answer onscreen.
Use arrow key to move to next question.

Level 4

Beginner 2 Hours
Medium 1 Hour
Advanced 30 Minutes

Additional Challenge

Set it to display questions and answer options. Player to press 1 2 or 3. Award point if correct.

Points

In Time 40
Additional 20

Notes on Approaching This Challenge

You'll need a suitable ds structure or array to hold the data. You'll need keypresses to change a value, while keeping it in valid range.

B. Tyers, *GameMaker: Studio 100 Programming Challenges*, DOI 10.1007/978-1-4842-2644-5_33

Guide

You can open a file with:

```
file=file_text_open_read("questions.txt");
```

You can read a string from a text file:

```
example=file_text_read_string(file);
```

You can read an integer:

```
example_2=file_text_read_real(file);
```

You can move to the next line:

```
file_text_readln(file);
```

You can close a file:

```
file_text_close();
```

You can detect an arrow keypress:

```
if (keyboard_check_pressed(vk_left))
{ //do something}
```

You can compare two integer variables:

```
if int1==int2
{//do something}
```

You can add a value to an array:

```
example_array[2,2]=value;
```

You can get contents from an array:

```
data=example_array[2,2];
```

CHALLENGE 34

Onscreen Keyboard

Challenge Outline

To create a keyboard where the user can click on a letter and add this to a string. Also include an enter key. Each key should be a separate object - do this manually or create buttons using code.

Level 3

Beginner 3 Hours
Medium 1 Hour
Advanced 30 Minutes

Additional Challenge

Allow entry of UPPER and lowercase letters and special characters.

Points

In Time 30
Additional 20

Notes on Approaching This Challenge

You'll need a button sprite for each letter (the same sprite can be used). You'll need to add each click letter to a string.

B. Tyers, *GameMaker: Studio 100 Programming Challenges*, DOI 10.1007/978-1-4842-2644-5_34

Guide

For each key you'll need a variable set, for example:

```
letter="A";
```

You can check if a left mouse button is clicked over a key:

```
if mouse_check_button_pressed(mb_left) && position_meeting(mouse_x,mouse_y,id)
{
        //do something
}
```

You can add a letter to a string:

```
global.message+=letter;
```

You can draw the letter over a button, but remember this will change formatting alignment for all future text unless set again as needed:

```
draw_set_halign(fa_center);
draw_text(x, y, letter);
```

There are various ways to create each button:

A separate object for each letter.

Multiple instances of the same object, making use of creation code that you can apply in the room editor, by right-clicking over object instance and selecting this option.

Create each button using GML.

CHALLENGE 35

Create a Drivable Tank That Leaves Tyre Tracks

Challenge Outline

Create a tank that can be moved using the keyboard. When it moves, place some tyre tracks that stay for a few seconds.

Level 2

Beginner 1 Hour
Medium 40 Minutes
Advanced 15 Minutes

Additional Challenge

Cause the tyre tracks to slowly fade away.

Points

In Time 20
Additional 20

Notes on Approaching This Challenge

You'll need two objects: one for the tank and one for the tyre tracks. You can use A D keys to rotate the tank and W to create some speed. You'll need some kind of timer to place tracks spaced out evenly. Also you'll need a timer to destroy tyre tracks after a given amount of time.

B. Tyers, *GameMaker: Studio 100 Programming Challenges*, DOI 10.1007/978-1-4842-2644-5_35

Guide

You can rotate an object, for example:

```
if keyboard_check(ord('A'))
{
        image_angle+=2;
        direction=image_angle
}
```

You can add speed:

```
if keyboard_check(ord('W'))
{
   speed+=0.5;
}
```

You can add friction:

```
speed-=0.2;
```

You can create an alarm:

```
alarm[0]=room_speed*5;
```

You can create an instance and set the angle:

```
tyre=instance_create(x,y,obj_tyre);//create a tyre
tyre.image_angle=direction;
```

You can destroy an instance:

```
instance_destroy();
```

CHALLENGE 36

Parallax Background

Challenge Outline

Combine a number of backgrounds to create a parallax effect. Have a player object that can move up and down. If the player object isn't being moved, slowly move it toward the middle. When moving up or down, rotate the sprite in the direction it's moving. Base the parallax on the player's y position.

Level 2

Beginner 1 Hour
Medium 40 Minutes
Advanced 25 Minutes

Additional Challenge

Allow zooming in and out of the player using middle mouse scroll button.

Points

In Time 20
Additional 20

Notes on Approaching This Challenge

Add each background through the room editor's background tab. Keep track of the y position of the player object and use this for the parallax effect.

B. Tyers, *GameMaker: Studio 100 Programming Challenges*, DOI 10.1007/978-1-4842-2644-5_36

Guide

You can detect keypresses and make an object move. For example:

```
if (keyboard_check(ord('W')))
{
        y-=5;
}
```

You can rotate an object:

```
image_angle=value;
```

You can gradually increase a variable:

```
y=y+0.1;
```

You can test a value:

```
if y>200
{
        y-=0.1;
}
```

You can set the y value of a created background:

```
background_y[1] = view_yview[0]+value;
```

Where value could be positive or negative.

CHALLENGE 37

Click the Ghost

Challenge Outline

To create a ghost that randomly appears at different positions. The player gets points by clicking on it. Use a single image or an animated sprite (in resources).

Level 1

Beginner 30 Minutes

Medium 20 Minutes

Advanced 8 Minutes

Additional Challenge

Make the object fade in when it appears and fade out when it disappears.

Points

In Time 10

Additional 20

Notes on Approaching This Challenge

For this challenge you'll need to make the object move to random positions and detect mouse clicks over an object.

B. Tyers, *GameMaker: Studio 100 Programming Challenges*, DOI 10.1007/978-1-4842-2644-5_37

Guide

You can make an object move to random positions using:

```
x=random(room_width);
y=random(room_height);
```

You can detect when a mouse is clicked over an object:

```
if position_meeting(mouse_x,mouse_y,id) && mouse_check_button_pressed(mb_left)
{
    //do something
}
```

You can set the image index and speed using:

```
image_index=0;
image_speed=0.5;
```

You can also check which sub-image an object's sprite is on:

```
if floor(image_index)==29
{
//do something
}
```

CHALLENGE 38

Particle Fire Effect

Challenge Outline

To create a fireplace effect using GM's particle system. Sprites that you can use for this project are in the resources pack.

Level 4

Beginner 3 Hours
Medium 1 Hour
Advanced 30 Minutes

Additional Challenge

Additionally create a smoke system above the fire.

Points

In Time 40
Additional 20

Notes on Approaching This Challenge

GM has a powerful particle system that can create a range of gorgeous effects. First up you'll need to create a particle system and set its attributes - such as how it looks, how it moves, and how long it lasts. You'll then need to make an emitter and then reference that to display the effects.

B. Tyers, *GameMaker: Studio 100 Programming Challenges*, DOI 10.1007/978-1-4842-2644-5_38

Guide

You can create a system:

```
global.partsys_fire = part_system_create();
```

You can set up a particle:

```
global.part_fire = part_type_create();
```

You can set how it looks:

```
part_type_sprite(global.part_fire,spr_fire,0,0,1);
part_type_size(global.part_fire,1.5,3,-.05,0);
part_type_orientation(global.part_fire,0,360,2,0,0);
part_type_color2(global.part_fire,c_orange,c_red);
part_type_alpha3(global.part_fire,1,1,0);
part_type_blend(global.part_fire,1);
```

how it moves:

```
part_type_direction(global.part_fire,85,95,0,0);
part_type_speed(global.part_fire,2,10,-.1,0);
```

how long it lasts for:

```
part_type_life(global.part_fire,25,35);
```

set an emitter:

```
my_emitter = part_emitter_create(global.partsys_fire);
part_emitter_region(global.partsys_fire,my_emitter,-50,850,450,500,ps_shape_rectangle,
ps_distr_linear);
```

You can cause the emitter to create a burst of particles:

```
part_emitter_burst(global.partsys_fire,my_emitter,global.part_fire,10);
```

CHALLENGE 39

Bubble Sort

Challenge Outline

Allow the user to enter 10 names and sort them in order using a bubble sort algorithm. Bubble sort is where you compare values and swap if one has a bigger value than the other. You repeat this until all is in order. If you compare values however many times there are elements minus 1, then it will be in order.

Level 2

Beginner 2 Hours

Medium 1 Hour

Advanced 30 Minutes

Additional Challenge

Display the sorting visually, slowly.

Points

In Time 20

Additional 20

Notes on Approaching This Challenge

You'll need some kind of data structure to hold the names; a ds list or an array is suitable.

You'll need types of loops to retrieve and compare values at certain positions.

B. Tyers, *GameMaker: Studio 100 Programming Challenges*, DOI 10.1007/978-1-4842-2644-5_39

Guide

You can create a ds list with:

```
names=ds_list_create();
```

You can add values to a list:

```
ds_list_add(names,"Mike","Steve","Chris");
```

You can create a for loop, which, for example, would loop 1 through 9 inclusive:

```
for (i = 1; i < 10; i += 1)
{
        //do something
}
```

You can get a value from a `ds_list` using an accessor, for example:

```
value=names[|5];
```

You can compare values and do something:

```
if value1>value2
{
        //do something
}
```

CHALLENGE 40

Unlockable Levels Select Screen

Challenge Outline

To create 5 buttons that can be locked or unlocked. Show its current state using different sub-images. Use a single object for all buttons. For testing purposes, the left and right arrow keys change the current level variable.

Level 2

Beginner 1 Hour
Medium 30 Minutes
Advanced 20 Minutes

Additional Challenge

Make the highest unlocked level sprite zoom in and out.

Points

In Time 20
Additional 20

Notes on Approaching This Challenge

Suitable sprites are in the resources pack. You'll need to use instance and global variables for this. You also need to use some basic drawing code.

B. Tyers, *GameMaker: Studio 100 Programming Challenges*, DOI 10.1007/978-1-4842-2644-5_40

Guide

You can check for keypress release:

```
if (keyboard_check_released(vk_left))
{
        // do something
}
```

You can set the value of an image index, that is, the sub-image to use:

```
image_index=0;
```

You can create a global variable:

```
global.example=2;
```

You can test 2 variables:

```
if value1>=value2
{
        //Do something
}
```

You can add creation code by right-clicking an object in the room editor.
You can show a message:

```
show_message("Message");
```

CHALLENGE 41

Moon Lander AI

Challenge Outline

To create a moon lander vehicle at the position where the left mouse button is clicked.
Program the lander so that it can hover and move left and right on its own. It needs to land on a target at the bottom of the screen. When moving it should carry some momentum.

Level 3

Beginner 2 Hours

Medium 1 Hour

Advanced 30 Minutes

Additional Challenge

Randomly place some asteroids in the middle of the room that the lander must avoid.

Points

In Time 30

Additional 20

Notes on Approaching This Challenge

This challenge will need some planning, with lots of math. This is a great introduction to an AI system. You can use vspeed and hspeed for this.

B. Tyers, *GameMaker: Studio 100 Programming Challenges*, DOI 10.1007/978-1-4842-2644-5_41

Guide

You can create an instance of an object when the mouse button is released:

```
if mouse_check_button_released(mb_left)
{
    instance_create(mouse_x,mouse_y,obj_ship);
}
```

You can set vspeed (vertical) and hspeed (horizontal), which can be positive or negative:

```
hspeed=3;
```

You can simulate friction:

```
hspeed=hspeed*0.99;
```

You may want to set hspeed and / or vspeed to 0 if below a certain threshold:

```
if hspeed<0.05 and hspeed>-0.05 hspeed=0;
```

You can check x and y positions against another instance, which works if only one instance is present:

```
if obj_platform.x<x
{
        //do something
}
```

You can use the abs function to get the absolute value of a variable, that is, chop off any negative value. For example:

```
new_value=abs(value);
```

You can check for a collision:

```
if place_meeting(x,y,obj_platform)
{ //do something }
```

CHALLENGE 42

Dodge the Barrels

Challenge Outline

To create a horizontally movable player, and barrels that fall from the top of the screen. Increase the frequency of the barrels as the game progresses.

Level 1

Beginner 1 Hour

Medium 25 Minutes

Advanced 8 Minutes

Additional Challenge

Create some burning barrels with fire and smoke effects.

Points

In Time 10

Additional 20

Notes on Approaching This Challenge

You'll need at least 2 objects for this. Player movement should be relatively easy. You'll need some kind of timing system to spawn the barrels. When barrels are created you'll need to make them fall.

B. Tyers, *GameMaker: Studio 100 Programming Challenges*, DOI 10.1007/978-1-4842-2644-5_42

Guide

Simple movement can be done, for example:

```
if (keyboard_check(vk_left))  {x-=5;}
```

A count can be created:

```
count=200;
```

An alarm can be set:

```
alarm[0]=count;
```

A count can be reduced, and you may wish to limit this. For example:

```
count-=1;
```

You may wish to limit the lower value of count. One method is:

```
if count<5 count=5;
```

You can set a random value based on the width of the room:

```
value=random(room_width);
```

You can create an instance of an object:

```
instance_create(x_pos,y_pos,object_name);
```

You can make an instance move:

```
motion_set(270,3);
```

You can destroy an instance when leaving the room:

```
if y>room_height instance_destroy();
```

You can check for a collision:

```
if place_meeting(x,y,object)
{
        //do something
}
```

CHALLENGE 43

Convert Celsius to Fahrenheit

Challenge Outline

User enters a temperature in degrees C, and the program converts this to degrees Fahrenheit.

Level 1

Beginner 30 Minutes
Medium 20 Minutes
Advanced 8 Minutes

Additional Challenge

Draw this graphically on a thermometer.

Points

In Time 10
Additional 20

Notes on Approaching This Challenge

To convert C to F you multiply by 9, divide by 5, then add 32.

B. Tyers, *GameMaker: Studio 100 Programming Challenges*, DOI 10.1007/978-1-4842-2644-5_43

Guide

You can get data in using:

```
variable_name=get_integer("Question Text",0);
```

You can display a variable:

```
show_message(variable_name);
```

Once you have a variable you can apply mathematical operators. For example + - * /:

```
new_variable=old_variable*2;
```

CHALLENGE 44

Dart Board Game

Challenge Outline

To allow the player to throw darts at a dart board. A mouse click starts each throw by making the dart move around outer edge of board, and the next mouse click makes dart move across board. A final mouse to click throws the dart.
Player start at 501 and the score reduces according to the position on the board. The player must finish with a double or outer bull's-eye.
Keep track of score and previous dart throws.

Level 5

Beginner 3 Hours
Medium 2 Hours
Advanced 1 Hour

Additional Challenge

Allow for between and 2 and 4 players. Each player gets 3 darts per go.
Display a graphical effect if a valid 180 is scored.

Points

In Time 50
Additional 20

Notes on Approaching This Challenge

You'll need to calculate angles and distances from a point (middle of bull's-eye) to where the dart lands. Calculate scoring position based on these values.

B. Tyers, *GameMaker: Studio 100 Programming Challenges*, DOI 10.1007/978-1-4842-2644-5_44

Guide

You can calculate the angle between two points:

```
angle=(point_direction(x1,y1,y2,y2);
```

As a dart board has 20 radial sections (so 18' for each section), you can find which one it lands in:

```
angle=(point_direction(x,y,obj_dart.x,obj_dart.y)+8) mod 360;
segment=angle div 18;
```

and get the value of that position:

```
if segment==0 pos=6;
```

You can calculate a distance to a point or an instance, for example obj_dart (if only one):

```
distance=distance_to_point(obj_dart.x,obj_dart.y);
```

You can then perform a test on the distance, for example, outside the main board area:

```
if distance>198
    {
        throw=0;
    }
```

Equally you can find if the dart lands on a double:

```
if distance>=178 && distance<=197
    {
        throw=pos*2;
        type="double";
    }
```

Simple ds_lists can be used for both score and previous throws can be used:

```
global.scores=ds_list_create();
ds_list_add(global.scores,score);
```

CHALLENGE 45

Calculate BMI

Challenge Outline

User to enter weight and height, calculate and display BMI. BMI is the weight in kilograms divided by height in meters squared.

Level 1

Beginner 30 Minutes

Medium 10 Minutes

Advanced 8 Minutes

Additional Challenge

Also display how much weight needs to be gained or lost for next BMI section.

Points

In Time 10

Additional 20

Notes on Approaching This Challenge

Just get the required data and perform the required calculation.

B. Tyers, *GameMaker: Studio 100 Programming Challenges*, DOI 10.1007/978-1-4842-2644-5_45

Guide

You can get an integer in, for example:

```
weight=get_integer("Weight In KG",0);
```

You can perform maths functions. ^ means to the power of, so:

```
value=10^2;
```

would set value as 100.

You can divide. For example:

```
var1=28;
var2=2;
answer=var1/var2;
```

would set answer as 14.

You can draw text and integer:

```
draw_text(100,100, "Answer is "+string(answer);
```

CHALLENGE 46

Colour Picker

Challenge Outline

Display a colour wheel onscreen and allow player to choose a colour.

Level 1

Beginner 1 Hour
Medium 30 Minutes
Advanced 12 Minutes

Additional Challenge

Allow user to draw up to 5 rectangles, each with a chosen colour.

Points

In Time 10
Additional 20

Notes on Approaching This Challenge

There are a few methods of getting the pixel colour at the mouse position; look in the manual and try to find them.

B. Tyers, *GameMaker: Studio 100 Programming Challenges*, DOI 10.1007/978-1-4842-2644-5_46

Guide

You can get the colour at the mouse's position:

```
my_colour=draw_getpixel(mouse_x,mouse_y);
```

You can then use this colour to draw something, such as a rectangle or a circle:

```
draw_set_colour(my_colour);
draw_circle(x,y,40,false);
```

CHALLENGE 47

10 Green Bottles

Challenge Outline

To display lyrics to the song, "10 Green Bottles." Use loops and variables to display the lyrics. This can be combined with challenge 19.

Level 3

Beginner 1 Hour
Medium 30 Minutes
Advanced 20 Minutes

Additional Challenge

Sync this to a music track.

Points

In Time 30
Additional 20

Notes on Approaching This Challenge

You'll need some kind of loop to count down from 10 to 1. You'll need to combine numbers and strings (by changing integers to strings). The repeated part of the song can be stored in strings. You can display each line using alarms and drawing, or create a message system (challenge 19) to buffer the lines.

B. Tyers, *GameMaker: Studio 100 Programming Challenges*, DOI 10.1007/978-1-4842-2644-5_47

Guide

You can combine a string and integer, for example if value=10 :

```
str="hello"+string(value);
```

You can make a for loop count down:

```
for (var bottles = 10; bottles > 1; bottles -= 1) { //do something}
```

You can do something based on a value, for example:

```
if bottles>1 { //do something}
```

You can set an alarm:

```
alarm[1]=room_speed*1;
```

You can draw text (a string in this case) at a position for example:

```
draw_text(400,300,string_to_draw);
```

You can create a ds list:

```
global.message=ds_list_create();
```

You can add to a ds list:

```
ds_list_add(global.message,string_to_add);
```

You can get the size of a ds list:

```
size=ds_list_size(global.message);
```

You can get the contents of an entry at a position in a ds list with:

```
to_draw=ds_list_find_value(global.message,0);
```

or

```
to_draw=global.message[|0];
```

You can delete at a position:

```
ds_list_delete(global.message,0);
```

CHALLENGE 48

English to Morse Code

Challenge Outline

Accept a string from a user and convert to Morse code and display on screen. Allow for letters only.

Level 2

Beginner 2 Hours

Medium 1 Hour

Advanced 40 Minutes

Additional Challenge

Allow for full punctuation. Give an option to output as audio.

Points

In Time 20

Additional 20

Notes on Approaching This Challenge

You'll need to get a string with the sentence the player wishes to transpose into Morse. Then get each letter in the string and add the correct Morse to another string.

B. Tyers, *GameMaker: Studio 100 Programming Challenges*, DOI 10.1007/978-1-4842-2644-5_48

Guide

You can get a string in:

```
source=get_string("Enter Sentence","");
```

Change all characters to uppercase, to make looking for letters easier:

```
source=string_upper(source);
```

Get the length of the string in characters:

```
source_length=string_length(source);
```

Create a loop:

```
for (var char = 1; char <= source_length+1; char += 1)//loop through characters
{
        //do something
}
```

Then test each letter, for example:

```
if letter=="A" add=".-/";
```

Or if a space " " is present, you can add spaces or a line break, for example:

```
if letter==" " add="#";
```

Then add this letter to your Morse string:

```
morse+=add;
```

CHALLENGE 49

Blitz Game Remake

Challenge Outline

Blitz was a popular game in the '80s. You have a plane that moves across the screen, gradually getting lower. The aim is to destroy the buildings below.

Level 1

Beginner 1 Hour

Medium 40 Minutes

Advanced 20 Minutes

Additional Challenge

Create a random cityscape for the buildings.

Points

In Time 10

Additional 20

Notes on Approaching This Challenge

You'll need 3 objects: a plane, bomb, and building block. On game start set the plane moving. When it reaches the side of the screen, wrap it and reduce its height. Create a moving bomb on mouse click if this collides with a building block, and then destroy the block and itself.

B. Tyers, *GameMaker: Studio 100 Programming Challenges*, DOI 10.1007/978-1-4842-2644-5_49

Guide

You can set the player moving with:

```
motion_set(0,4);
```

You can create a bomb on a mouse click:

```
if mouse_check_button_pressed(mb_left) && global.can_shoot
{
        instance_create(x,y+16,obj_bomb);
global.can_shoot=false;
}
```

On a bomb collision with a building block:

```
with (other) instance_destroy();
global.can_shoot=true;
instance_destroy();
```

You can wrap around the room and reduce the height:

```
if x>1000
{
    y=y+16;
    x=-32;
}
```

CHALLENGE 50

Mini Golf Game Remake

Challenge Outline

Create a mini (crazy) golf game. Make the ball move toward the mouse position. Use the distance from ball to mouse as a reference for how fast the ball will travel. Create some objects that the player should navigate to get to the hole.

Level 1

Beginner 1 Hour
Medium 30 Minutes
Advanced 12 Minutes

Additional Challenge

Create this challenge using physics.

Points

In Time 10
Additional 20

Notes on Approaching This Challenge

You'll need some separate objects for the ball, walls, and hole. You'll need to use appropriate functions to find the distance and direction between ball and mouse. You'll need solid objects for ball and wall objects.

B. Tyers, *GameMaker: Studio 100 Programming Challenges*, DOI 10.1007/978-1-4842-2644-5_50

Guide

To make an object bounce, set the colliding object to solid and use this code in the collision event:

```
move_bounce_solid(true);
```

To get the distance from an instance to the mouse position use:

```
distance=distance_to_point(mouse_x,mouse_y);
```

To get a direction use:

```
dir=point_direction(x,y,mouse_x,mouse_y);
```

You can set the speed of an instance with:

```
speed=value;
```

You can gradually reduce speed in a Step Event:

```
speed*=0.8;
```

You can set the speed straight to 0 if it falls below a certain value:

```
if speed<0.5 speed=0;
```

CHALLENGE 51

Rock, Paper, Scissors Game Remake

Challenge Outline

Re-create the classic rock, paper, and scissors. The player competes against the computer. Allow keys R P S to make a selection. First to 10 points wins.

Level 2

Beginner 1 Hour
Medium 40 Minutes
Advanced 20 Minutes

Additional Challenge

At end of the game, show the results of all goes and who won which go.

Points

In Time 20
Additional 20

Notes on Approaching This Challenge

You'll need some kind of input to allow player to make a choice. The computer will need to choose 1 of 3 options for its guess. Then compare the player's and computer's selection, and apply points accordingly. After each play, check if player or computer has reached 10 points.

B. Tyers, *GameMaker: Studio 100 Programming Challenges*, DOI 10.1007/978-1-4842-2644-5_51

Guide

You can set initial starting variables, for example:

```
player_wins=0;
```

You can get a player's guess:

```
guess=get_string("R P or S","");
```

You can change to uppercase:

```
guess=string_upper(guess);
```

You can change selection to a word:

```
if guess=="R" player_play="Rock";
```

You can get the computer to choose 1 2 or 3 at random:

```
play=irandom_range(1,3);
```

then set a word from it:

```
if play=1 computer_play="Rock";
```

and compare player and computer:

```
if player_play="Rock" && computer_play=="Rock"
{
        //do something
}
```

More advanced users may wish to use enums as states instead of strings.
You can increase a value by 1:

```
draw++;
```

You can show a message:

```
show_message("This is a message");
```

CHALLENGE 52

Health Based on Distance

Challenge Outline

Place an object in the room, set health as 1000. Reduce health based on distance from object to mouse click.

Level 1

Beginner 30 Minutes
Medium 20 Minutes
Advanced 10 Minutes

Additional Challenge

Create some code to simulate mouse click at random positions.

Points

In Time 10
Additional 20

Notes on Approaching This Challenge

First get the player in the middle of the room; you can base this on room dimensions. When the mouse is clicked, use a suitable function to get the distance - use this value to reduce health.

B. Tyers, *GameMaker: Studio 100 Programming Challenges*, DOI 10.1007/978-1-4842-2644-5_52

Guide

You can set health at 1000:

```
health=1000;
```

You can get the middle point of the room, for example:

```
xx=room_width/2;
```

You can detect a global mouse click:

```
if mouse_check_button_released(mb_left)
{
        //do something
}
```

You can get the distance from self to another point:

```
distance=distance_to_point(xx,yy);
```

You can decrease a value by an amount:

```
amount=10;
value-=amount;
```

You can draw player and heath:

```
draw_self();
draw_text(20,20,"Health: "+string(health));
```

CHALLENGE 53

Tank Trax Game Remake

Challenge Outline

To remake a basic version of Tank Trax (like a gorilla, worms, angry bird type game).
Two players take turns trying to hit each other by firing their gun.
Power and bullet direction are set by the position of the mouse relative to the player.

Level 4

Beginner 2 Hours
Medium 1 Hour
Advanced 40 Minutes

Additional Challenge

Display and compensate for random wind each shot. Randomly generate terrain for each game.

Points

In Time 40
Additional 20

Notes on Approaching This Challenge

For this you'll need to use functions for finding distance and angles between mouse position and player. You'll need to update a moving object so it appears gravity is being applied.

B. Tyers, *GameMaker: Studio 100 Programming Challenges*, DOI 10.1007/978-1-4842-2644-5_53

Guide

One approach to calculating velocity of a bullet is:

```
strength=distance_to_point(mouse_x,mouse_y)/50;
```

The angle can be found using:

```
angle=point_direction(x,y,mouse_x,mouse_y);
```

A mouse click can found with:

```
if mouse_check_button_released(mb_left)
```

You can create a bullet and set its speed and angle:

```
bullet=instance_create(x,y,obj_bullet_1);
bullet.speed=strength;
bullet.direction=angle;
```

To keep track of whose go it is, you can use a global variable:

```
global.player=1;
```

and then run code, for example:

```
if global.player==1
{
//do something
global.player=2;
}
```

In a bullet's step event you can simulate gravity:

```
vspeed=vspeed+0.02;
```

In a bullet collision event with an opposing player:

```
show_message("player 1 wins");
game_restart();
```

CHALLENGE 54

Two Separate Views

Challenge Outline

For this challenge you'll need to create 2 objects and 2 views, with each view following a different object. Have the room size as 2000x2000 and each view as 400x400, shown side by side.
Note: GameMaker bases the window size on the first room run. To prevent any scaling issues, ensure all rooms have the same size or same ratio of width and height. In this can an initial splash room of 800x400 will set things up nicely:
room_goto(room_example);

Level 4

Beginner 2 Hours

Medium 1 Hour

Advanced 30 Minutes

Additional Challenge

If both objects are within 200 pixels of each other, change to a single view. If they proceed over this value, revert back to 2 separate views.

Points

In Time 40

Additional 20

Notes on Approaching This Challenge

This can easily be done using the room's view tab. Try to do this solely in code.

B. Tyers, *GameMaker: Studio 100 Programming Challenges*, DOI 10.1007/978-1-4842-2644-5_54

Guide

You can set and enable views in room editor, also in code if needed:

```
view_enabled[0] = true;
view_visible[0] = true;
```

You can set the view size (the size where the view will be taken from):

```
view_wview[0]=400;
view_hview[0]=400;
```

You can set the port position (where you'll draw the port):

```
view_xport[0]=0;//set position of port
view_yport[0]=0;
```

You can set the width and height of the port:

```
view_wport[0]=400;//set size of port
view_hport[0]=400;
```

You can set the view to follow an object:

```
view_object[0]=obj_player_1;//set object to follow
```

And set the border amount when following:

```
view_hborder[0] = view_wview[0] / 2;
view_vborder[0] = view_hview[0] / 2;
```

For following a second object and new view port you can reference it using [1] instead of [0]. Of course, change this position where the port is drawn, for example:

```
view_xport[1]=400;
```

CHALLENGE 55

Word Typing Game

Challenge Outline

To display a word at random on the screen. Player is to type word before time runs out. If player types in time, award points, reset timer, and create a new word. If player does not type in time, reduce points, reset timer, and display a new word.

Level 3

Beginner 3 Hours
Medium 1 Hour
Advanced 30 Minutes

Additional Challenge

Increase the word length as the player's score increases.

Points

In Time 30
Additional 20

Notes on Approaching This Challenge

You'll need a suitable data structure to hold the words, and choose one at random for each game. Then compare that to the string held in the computer's memory. Add points and time can be done with basic variables.

B. Tyers, *GameMaker: Studio 100 Programming Challenges*, DOI 10.1007/978-1-4842-2644-5_55

Guide

A ds list can be created and populated:

```
words=ds_list_create();
ds_list_add(words,"ham","eggs","potato","cheese","pizza", "chocolate");
```

You can get the number of elements in a ds list:

```
size=ds_list_size(words);
```

You can choose 1 entry at random (-1 is used as a ds list starts at position 0):

```
word=words[|irandom_range(0,size-1)];
```

The variable `keyboard_string` holds the most recently types letter, which can be cleared with:

```
keyboard_string="";
```

You can compare `keyboard_string` with another string, for example:

```
if keyboard_string==word {//do something}
```

You can use health as timer:

```
timer=100;
```

and reduce each step:

```
timer-=1;
```

and do something if it reaches 0:

```
if timer==0
{ //do something; health=100;}
```

You can draw the current string in `keyboard_string`:

```
draw_text(100,150,"Word Typed: "+keyboard_string);
```

CHALLENGE 56

■ ■ ■

Destructible Terrain

Challenge Outline

To create a terrain that can be destroyed (have holes cut in it) when hit by an object.
Try combining with challenge 53.

Level 5

Beginner 3 Hours
Medium 1 Hour
Advanced 30 Minutes

Additional Challenge

Adapt the cut size depending on how fast the impacting object is traveling.

Points

In Time 50
Additional 20

Notes on Approaching This Challenge

For this challenge you'll need to use surfaces. You can create a surface draw onto it and then save it. You can then draw onto this surface and remove what you have drawn to leave a hole.

B. Tyers, *GameMaker: Studio 100 Programming Challenges*, DOI 10.1007/978-1-4842-2644-5_56

Guide

You can create a surface:

```
surface = surface_create(w,h);
surface_set_target(surface);
draw_sprite(spr_terrain,-1,0,0);
surface_reset_target();
```

Then make a sprite from this:

```
spr=sprite_create_from_surface(surface,0,0,w,h,true,true,0,0);
```

On collision we can set the surface:

```
surface_set_target(surface);
```

Set drawing colour and draw a circle that is filled in:

```
draw_set_color(c_white);
draw_circle(xpos,ypos, radius, false);
```

Next, reset it, which will remove the circle and leave a hole

```
surface_reset_target();
```

Delete the current sprite, but you must assign a new sprite first:
Sprite_image

```
sprite_index(spr_new);
sprite_delete(spr);
```

Then create a new sprite

```
spr=sprite_create_from_surface(surface,0,0,w,h,1,1,0,0);
```

Finally apply a sprite:

```
sprite_index=spr;
```

CHALLENGE 57

Duck Hunt Game Remake

Challenge Outline

Duck Hunt is a classic game from the 1980s. A duck flies across the screen and the aim is to shoot it down. You should control a gunsight and get points if you fire (press mouse button) when over a duck.

Level 1

Beginner 1 Hour
Medium 30 Minutes
Advanced 15 Minutes

Additional Challenge

Create a dead duck that falls when successfully shot. Award more points depending on how close to the middle of duck the player shoots.

Points

In Time 10
Additional 20

Notes on Approaching This Challenge

You'll need 2 objects: a duck and player gunsight that also spawns more ducks. Try to set the starting position of each duck at random positions and give some variation in movement, speed, and direction.

B. Tyers, *GameMaker: Studio 100 Programming Challenges*, DOI 10.1007/978-1-4842-2644-5_57

Guide

You can assign a gun sprite to the player and make it move with:

```
x=mouse_x; y=mouse_y;
```

You can check if player is both shooting and over the duck object:

```
if mouse_check_button_pressed(mb_left) && position_meeting(x,y,obj_duck)//if mouse pressed
{
    score+=10;
   inst=instance_position(x,y,obj_duck);
    with (inst) { instance_destroy();}
}
```

You can set an alarm to spawn a duck:

```
alarm[0]=100+random(room_speed*3);
```

You can make a duck move, for example left at a speed of 4:

```
motion_set(180,4);
```

You can spawn the duck at a random y position:

```
y=irandom_range(100,room_height-100);
```

You can detect if the duck is off the screen and destroy it:

```
if y<-50
{ instance_destroy();}
```

CHALLENGE 58

Keep Player in View

Challenge Outline

To allow the view to follow a player object, keeping a border while moving. Allow moving the player by WSAD and keep a border of 250.

Level 1

Beginner 40 Minutes
Medium 20 Minutes
Advanced 10 Minutes

Additional Challenge

Create a view that keeps 2 player objects in the same view, by zooming in / out as required.

Points

In Time 10
Additional 20

Notes on Approaching This Challenge

For this challenge use code rather than the options in the room settings.

You can set the view size, enable it, and set it to follow an object with a border.

B. Tyers, *GameMaker: Studio 100 Programming Challenges*, DOI 10.1007/978-1-4842-2644-5_58

Guide

For movement code you can use:

```
if (keyboard_check(ord('A')))  {x-=5;}
if (keyboard_check(ord('D')))  {x+=5;}
if (keyboard_check(ord('W')))  {y-=5;}
if (keyboard_check(ord('S')))  {y+=5;}
```

You can set view size:

```
view_wview[0]=600;
view_hview[0]=600;
```

You can enable a view:

```
view_enabled[0] = true;
```

You can make a view visible:

```
view_visible[0] = true;
```

You can set the border for following an object:

```
view_hborder[0]=250;
view_vborder[0]=250;
```

and assign an object to follow:

```
view_object[0]=obj_player;
```

As GM bases the room window size on the first room, create a room room_init, set width and height to 800 and add an object with this code:

```
room_goto(room_example);
```

CHALLENGE 59

Fizz Buzz

Challenge Outline

Output numbers 1 to 50. If a number is a multiple of 3, display fizz. If a number is a multiple of 5, write buzz. If it is a multiple of 3 and 5, write fizzbuzz.

Level 2

Beginner 3 Hours

Medium 1 Hour

Advanced 30 Minutes

Additional Challenge

Use different font colours for fizz & buzz.

Points

In Time 20

Additional 20

Notes on Approaching This Challenge

You'll need some kind of loop to count up to 50. There is a mathematical function that returns the remainder when divided into another number. You'll also need to draw strings of the numbers or fizz / buzz.

B. Tyers, *GameMaker: Studio 100 Programming Challenges*, DOI 10.1007/978-1-4842-2644-5_59

Guide

You can create a loop to count up to a value, for example 10:

```
for (var count=1; count<11; count+=1)
{
//do something
}
```

You can find out if a number divides another wholly using mod for example 7 into 21:

```
if 21 mod 7==0
{
//do something
}
```

You can set a variable as a string:

```
string_example=string(46);
```

CHALLENGE 60

Calculate Numbers

Challenge Outline

Allow the user to enter two numbers - A and B - between 1 and 1000.
Calculate and display each of the following:
Which number is bigger
Multiply A by B
Divide the biggest by the smallest
Calculate biggest modulo the smallest
What A plus B is

Level 1

Beginner 1 Hour

Medium 30 Minutes

Advanced 12 Minutes

Additional Challenge

Create an onscreen keyboard to allow appropriate data to be entered.

Points

In Time 10

Additional 20

Notes on Approaching This Challenge

This is very basic. Calculate each as a new variable and draw onto the screen.

B. Tyers, *GameMaker: Studio 100 Programming Challenges*, DOI 10.1007/978-1-4842-2644-5_60

Guide

You can get a user to enter data, for example:

```
a=get_integer("Enter Number ",0);
```

You can then perform code on this, for example, check if A is bigger than B:

```
if a>b
{
    text="A is bigger";
}
```

To divide use:

```
divided=b/a;
```

To get a modulus:

```
modulus=a mod b;
```

and similar for addition and multiplication.

You can draw using:

```
draw_text(20,40,text);
draw_text(20,80,"Biggest Divided By Smallest "+string(divided));
```

CHALLENGE 61

Particle Trail Effect

Challenge Outline

To create a particle trail when an object moves.

Level 1

Beginner 40 Minutes
Medium 20 Minutes
Advanced 10 Minutes

Additional Challenge

Create a stream of particles in the opposite direction of object movement.

Points

In Time 10
Additional 20

Notes on Approaching This Challenge

This can be done using either objects or a particle system. An extra 10 points for using the particle system.

B. Tyers, *GameMaker: Studio 100 Programming Challenges*, DOI 10.1007/978-1-4842-2644-5_61

Guide

You can make an instance move to the mouse position with:

```
x=mouse_x;
y=mouse_y;
```

You can create an instance of a particle object:

```
part = instance_create(x,y,obj_particle);
part.vspeed = 1;
part.gravity = 0.1;
part.delta = 0.1;
```

You can fade out the instance:

```
image_alpha -= delta;
```

and destroy it if invisible:

```
if image_alpha <= 0 instance_destroy();
```

CHALLENGE 62

Draw a Rectangle and Calculate Area and Perimeter

Challenge Outline

Allow the user to click 2 places in a room. Draw a rectangle and calculate and display its area and perimeter. (Clicks for top left and bottom right)

Level 1

Beginner 1 Hour

Medium 20 Minutes

Advanced 10 Minutes

Additional Challenge

Allow user to click twice to make a first rectangle, then twice again for a second rectangle. Highlight any overlapping area and display its area and perimeter.

Points

In Time 10

Additional 20

Notes on Approaching This Challenge

For this challenge you'll need to store the x and y positions when a mouse button is clicked and then perform some basic math on these values. You may need to use a counter to track how many clicks there have been. To display the results you can use basic text drawing.

B. Tyers, *GameMaker: Studio 100 Programming Challenges*, DOI 10.1007/978-1-4842-2644-5_62

Guide

You can detect a mouse button released:

```
if mouse_check_button_released(mb_left)
{
        //do something
}
```

You can store the position of a mouse. For example:

```
x1=mouse_x;
```

You can create values:

```
a=5;
b=8;
```

You can add them:

```
c=a+b;
```

You can multiply them:

```
d=a*b;
```

You can draw them with text:

```
draw_text(50,50, "Answer "+string(d));
```

You can keep track of how many clicks. For example, in the create event:

```
click=0;
```

and in a step event:

```
if mouse_check_button_released(mb_left) && click==0
{
x1=mouse_x; y1= mouse_y; click+=1;
}
```

CHALLENGE 63

Tower Defense Game

Challenge Outline

Create a basic tower defense game, with enemies that follow a path.
Have a selection of turrets that the player can purchase.
Turrets should have a range set, and shoot at enemies within that range.
Player to buy and place turrets if they have enough cash.
Resources are available in the downloads.

Level 4

Beginner 5 Hours
Medium 3 Hours
Advanced 2 Hours

Additional Challenge

Add: Blood splatters, a menu with unlockable levels, a save / load system; allow turret upgrades with different sprite and power for bullets.

Points

In Time 40
Additional 20

Notes on Approaching This Challenge

You'll need a control object to spawn the terrain blocks. You'll need to choose a "starting" position for the first grass instance, draw it, draw 3 dirt tiles underneath (or to the bottom of the room) and then (if space) place stones to the bottom of the room.

Then proceed to the next grass object basing it on a random range +/- 3 positions from the previous grass block. Repeat for the width of the room.

B. Tyers, *GameMaker: Studio 100 Programming Challenges*, DOI 10.1007/978-1-4842-2644-5_63

Guide

You can choose a previously set path at random:

```
path_start(choose(path_1_1,path_1_2),2,path_action_restart,true);
```

You can check if the player has enough cash for a purchase:

```
if global.cash>=price available=true; else available=false;
```

You can check whether an item is available:

```
if mouse_check_button_released(mb_left) && position_meeting(x, y, obj_turret_1_menu) &&
selected=0
{
    if global.cash>=50
    {
        selected=1;
        cost=50;
        scr_sound(snd_weapon_selected);
    }
    else scr_sound(snd_not_enough_cash);
}
```

You can place instances of obj_place where turrets can be located. Then use this:

```
if selected>=1 && mouse_check_button_released(mb_left) && position_meeting(x, y, obj_place)
{
    if selected==1
    {
        nearest=instance_nearest(x,y,obj_place);
        instance_create(nearest.x,nearest.y,obj_turret_1);
        global.cash-=cost;
        selected=0;
        with nearest instance_destroy();

    }
    if selected==2
    {
        nearest=instance_nearest(x,y,obj_place);
        instance_create(nearest.x,nearest.y,obj_turret_2);
        global.cash-=cost;
        selected=0;
        with nearest instance_destroy();

    }
    if selected==3
    {
        nearest=instance_nearest(x,y,obj_place);
        instance_create(nearest.x,nearest.y,obj_turret_3);
        global.cash-=cost;
```

```
        selected=0;
        with nearest instance_destroy();

    }
}
```

You can check if something is in range and fire a bullet:

```
if distance_to_object(target)<range
{
    if level==0
    {
        bullet=instance_create(x+lengthdir_x(30, image_angle),y+lengthdir_y(30,
        image_angle),obj_bullet);
        bullet.image_angle=direction;
        bullet.direction=direction;
        bullet.speed=6;
        bullet.source=id;
        bullet.range=range;
        bullet.strength=50+(level*50);
        flash=instance_create(x+lengthdir_x(30, image_angle),y+lengthdir_y(30,
        image_angle),obj_flash);
        flash.image_angle=direction;
    }

}
```

In a Collision Event you can check for a collision and reduce hp:

```
if other.target=id
{
    hp-=other.strength;
    with (other) instance_destroy();
    scr_sound(snd_hit);
}
```

CHALLENGE 64

Drop the Coin AKA Plinko (Arcade Style)

Challenge Outline

To drop a coin from the top that bounces off pins to reach the bottom. Award points depending on which section it lands in.

Level 3

Beginner 2 Hours

Medium 1 Hour

Advanced 30 Minutes

Additional Challenge

Create this using GameMaker's physics engine.

Points

In Time 30

Additional 20

Notes on Approaching This Challenge

You'll need a ball (coin), wall, and a peg object. You can set the coin moving down on creation and set it to bounce off solid objects. You can use collision events to check if coin has landed in a scoring section. You'll need some spawning / control object to create the coin where the mouse is clicked.

B. Tyers, *GameMaker: Studio 100 Programming Challenges*, DOI 10.1007/978-1-4842-2644-5_64

Guide

You can set the coin moving;

```
motion_set(270,0.5);
gravity_direction = 270;
gravity=1;
```

With collision with solid objects (collision event):

```
move_bounce_solid(true);
var rand_direction=irandom_range(-3,3);
direction+=rand_direction;
```

You can change the position of the spawning controller:

```
x=mouse_x;
```

On mouse button released event:

```
instance_create(x,50,obj_ball);
```

To add to the score, use a collision event with the coin, and for example:

```
score+=10;
with (other) instance_destroy();
```

CHALLENGE 65

Calculate the Nth Result of Fibonacci Sequence

Challenge Outline

The user enters a number (up to 50). The program calculates the nth result of the Fibonacci sequence. The sequence goes: 1, 1, 2, 3, 5, 8, 13, 21, 34 and continues where the new number is the result of the previous 2 values.

Level 2

Beginner 30 Minutes
Medium 15 Minutes
Advanced 6 Minutes

Additional Challenge

Create an onscreen keyboard to allow appropriate data to be entered.

Points

In Time 20
Additional 20

Notes on Approaching This Challenge

Once you've got a valid number from the user, this boils down to some basic math of adding and storing values.

B. Tyers, *GameMaker: Studio 100 Programming Challenges*, DOI 10.1007/978-1-4842-2644-5_65

Guide

You can get the user to enter a numerical value:

```
sequence=get_integer("Enter a number",0);
```

You can create a basic for loop:

```
for (var loop=0; loop<=sequence; loop++ )
{
        //do something
}
```

You can define array variables:

```
data[0]=1;
data[1]=1;
```

You can add variables

```
data[2]=data[0]+data[1];
```

You can show a variable as a message:

```
show_message(data[5]);
```

CHALLENGE 66

Distance from Object to Mouse

Challenge Outline

Create an object whose instances calculate and display its distance and direction from the mouse cursor.

Level 1

Beginner 12 Minutes
Medium 8 Minutes
Advanced 4 Minutes

Additional Challenge

Allow a mouse click to add and remove instances.

Points

In Time 10
Additional 20

Notes on Approaching This Challenge

Just get the distance and angle using appropriate scripts.

B. Tyers, *GameMaker: Studio 100 Programming Challenges*, DOI 10.1007/978-1-4842-2644-5_66

Guide

You can get the distance and angle:

```
dist=distance_to_point(mouse_x,mouse_y);
angle=point_direction(x,y,mouse_x,mouse_y)
```

and draw these variables:

```
draw_text(x,y-40,"Distance "+string(dist));
draw_text(x,y-60,"Direction "+string(angle));
```

CHALLENGE 67

Convert Decimal to Binary, Oct, Hex, and Roman

Challenge Outline

To create scripts that convert a decimal entry to other bases.

Level 5

Beginner 3 Hours
Medium 1 Hour
Advanced 30 Minutes

Additional Challenge

Allow conversion to base 4 and base 12.

Points

In Time 50
Additional 20

Notes on Approaching This Challenge

There are two main approaches to this challenge.

You could bitwise operators for the hard approach.

You can also achieve using basic math operators such as + - * / div and mod.

B. Tyers, *GameMaker: Studio 100 Programming Challenges*, DOI 10.1007/978-1-4842-2644-5_67

Guide

For an example we will look at converting a number to base 8.

Let's use the number 29 as an example.

First we want to get how many times 8 goes into 29.

We can do this with:

```
times= num div 8;
```

which would give a result of 3.

Then we need the remainder of 8 going into 29, we can use:

```
remainder= num mod 8;
```

which would give a result of 5.

Joining these together in sequence we get 35, so the answer is 35.

If `times` gives an answer above 7 you would need to apply the process again recursively to get the true value.

A similar approach can be used on other bases.

CHALLENGE 68

■ ■ ■

Text in X Box

Challenge Outline

To accept a sentence and then redraw with Xs around it. For example:
XXXXXXXXXXX
Xhello worldX
XXXXXXXXXXX

Level 2

Beginner 40 Minutes
Medium 20 Minutes
Advanced 10 Minutes

Additional Challenge

Create a visual effect of having the Xs rotate around the sentence.

Points

In Time 10
Additional 20

Notes on Approaching This Challenge

You'll need to get the length of the sentence in characters and use this to make a string of Xs.

You can then combine this with the original sentence, adding a leading and trailing X. This is easiest when using a mono-spaced font, though using a non mono-spaced font is possible, albeit a bit harder to implement.

B. Tyers, *GameMaker: Studio 100 Programming Challenges*, DOI 10.1007/978-1-4842-2644-5_68

Guide

You can get a sentence in:

```
sentence=get_string("Sentence","");
```

You can get its length in characters:

```
length=string_length(sentence);
```

You can make a loop:

```
for (var i=1; i<=length+2; i++)
{
    //do something
}
```

You can add to an existing string, for example:

```
output+="X";
```

Once a font has been added, you can assign it with:

```
draw_set_font(font_example);
```

You can draw the output:

```
draw_text(100,100,output);
```

CHALLENGE 69

Frogger Game Remake

Challenge Outline

To re-create the classic game Frogger. You control a frog. First you need to get past a busy road, then navigate floating logs. Finally you need to reach the goal without being eaten by the crocodile.

Level 2

Beginner 2 Hours

Medium 1 Hour

Advanced 30 Minutes

Additional Challenge

Create an AI system that successfully completes the level.

Points

In Time 20

Additional 20

Notes on Approaching This Challenge

You'll need a frog controlled by arrow keys. You'll need some cars that move left and right, and wraps around screen. You'll need logs that move left and right, and also wrap around the room. You'll need a crocodile that randomly jumps positions.

You'll need collision detection to check if player collides with a car, is on a moving log, has fallen in water, has reached a goal, or collided with the crocodile.

B. Tyers, *GameMaker: Studio 100 Programming Challenges*, DOI 10.1007/978-1-4842-2644-5_69

Guide

You can control the frog using keypresses, for example:

```
if (keyboard_check(vk_left))  {x-=5;}
```

You can set a car or log moving. For example:

```
motion_set(180,2);
```

You can make an instance wrap around screen (left & right), based on the sprite origin being centered:

```
//wrap around room
if x<-(sprite_width/2) x=(room_width+1)+(sprite_width/2);
if x>(room_width+1)+(sprite_width/2) x=-(sprite_width/2);
```

You can detect a collision with a car or crocodile. For example:

```
if (place_meeting(x,y,obj_car_1)
{
show_message("You die"); game_restart();
}
```

You can make the frog move with a log. For example:

```
if (place_meeting(x,y,obj_wood_left))
{
    x-=3;
}
```

To make the crocodile jump to a random position, set up an alarm and use this code in the alarm event:

```
x=choose(200,400,600);
alarm[0]=3*room_speed;
```

CHALLENGE 70

Take a Screenshot

Challenge Outline

Create an object that allows you to take a screenshot and save it.
Set up for F to get the save path and take a screenshot.
Great for allowing sharing of your game on social media.

Level 2

Beginner 20 Minutes
Medium 10 Minutes
Advanced 5 Minutes

Additional Challenge

Take one screenshot every 1/10 of a second, which user can then make an animated GIF out of.

Points

In Time 10
Additional 20

Notes on Approaching This Challenge

Nothing fancy here, just keypress and a little code.

B. Tyers, *GameMaker: Studio 100 Programming Challenges*, DOI 10.1007/978-1-4842-2644-5_70

Guide

First up you'll need the user to enter a filename to save.

If you want the user to enter the name of the file you could use:

```
name=get_string("Enter File Name","";
```

Then add .png extension:

```
name+=".png";
```

This would limit to saving in the default path.

Using the following would allow saving outside the sandboxed file area:

```
to_save = get_save_filename("png|*.png", "");
```

You can grab a screenshot of window using:

```
screen_save("filename");
```

CHALLENGE 71

Slowly Change Direction

Challenge Outline

To make an object point in the direction of the mouse if it is within + / - 25 ° angle of the mouse position.

Level 2

Beginner 1 Hour
Medium 30 Minutes
Advanced 20 Minutes

Additional Challenge

Also make objects move slowly toward the mouse position, only if the angle is +/- 25 ° angle toward the mouse, changing direction slowly.

Points

In Time 10
Additional 20

Notes on Approaching This Challenge

This uses some complex math. Either you know it or you don't.

B. Tyers, *GameMaker: Studio 100 Programming Challenges*, DOI 10.1007/978-1-4842-2644-5_71

Guide

Here is an example usage to make the object slowly move (speed 4) toward the mouse position:

```
dir=point_direction(x,y,mouse_x,mouse_y);
direction = image_angle;
difference=angle_difference(image_angle, dir);
```

You can check that a value is within a range, for example, between -100 and 100:

```
if abs(angle)<=100
{
//do something
}
```

CHALLENGE 72

Pong Style Game Remake

Challenge Outline

To re-create the classic game of pong. Set it up for 2 players: player 1 using W and S to move, and player 2 using up and down arrows.

Level 1

Beginner 30 Minutes
Medium 20 Minutes
Advanced 10 Minutes

Additional Challenge

Create an AI for player 2, with the option to set its skill from 1 to 5.

Points

In Time 10
Additional 20

Notes on Approaching This Challenge

You'll need 4 objects: two player objects, a wall, and a pong ball. On the balls collision with the wall or player, you'll need to figure out how to make it change direction. For player movement set it so a keypress changes its y position. If the ball leaves left or right of screen, award a point, and reset the ball back to the middle of the screen and serve again.

B. Tyers, *GameMaker: Studio 100 Programming Challenges*, DOI 10.1007/978-1-4842-2644-5_72

Guide

For movement you can use, for example:

```
if (keyboard_check(ord('W')))  {y-=5;}
```

or

```
if (keyboard_check(vk_up))  {y-=5;}
```

On the ball's collision with the wall you can use the following to change direction:

```
vspeed*=-1;
```

and collision with player:

```
hspeed*=-1;
```

To start the ball moving:

```
motion_set(45,3);
```

You can detect the ball leaving screen to award a point, for example:

```
if x>room_width//check if off right of screen
{
    //do stuff player 1 wins
}
```

You can prevent player going off screen, say the bottom; this assumes that the origin is at the center of the sprite:

```
if  y>room_height-height y=room_height-height;
```

CHALLENGE 73

Shooting Gallery

Challenge Outline

Create a crosshair movable by the mouse. The left mouse button shoots a bullet. Have some ducks that pop up at random for a short time. Award a point if the player hits a duck with a bullet, while it is shown.

Level 2

Beginner 1 Hour
Medium 30 Minutes
Advanced 20 Minutes

Additional Challenge

Award 3 points if the duck is hit, reduce by 1 point if a duck is missed. Player to reach 50 points to win. Only allow the player a set amount of time to reach the target score.

Points

In Time 20
Additional 20

Notes on Approaching This Challenge

Ideally a sprite with 2 sub-images is useful here. You can have index 0 as duck showing and index 1 as not showing. You'll need some kind of timing system to show and not show the ducks. Alarms are ideal for this. You'll also need to check if a duck is hit by a bullet.

B. Tyers, *GameMaker: Studio 100 Programming Challenges*, DOI 10.1007/978-1-4842-2644-5_73

Guide

You can start an alarm using, for example:

```
alarm[0]=irandom(room_speed*3);
```

which sets an alarm with a random time of between 0 and 3 seconds.

You can stop a sprite from animating if it has more than 1 sub-image with:

```
image_speed=0;
```

And set which sub-image to show, for example 1:

```
image_index=1;
```

You can get the instance id at a position:

inst=instance_position(x, y, obj_duck);

Test it to make sure it has a value:

```
if inst!=noone
{
        //do something
}
```

Then check a value of inst:

```
if inst.image_index==0
{
        //do something
}
```

You can update an instance to the mouse's position:

```
x=mouse_x;
y=mouse_y;
```

CHALLENGE 74

How Many of Each Letter

Challenge Outline

To accept an alphabetical string and count how many of each letter are present. Display the results as text on the screen.

Level 3

Beginner 1 Hour

Medium 30 Minutes

Advanced 20 Minutes

Additional Challenge

To display graphically using a bar graph. Order the results from most to least. Allow processing of a TXT file.

Points

In Time 30

Additional 20

Notes on Approaching This Challenge

For this challenge you'll need to hone your array and loop handling skills. You'll also need to make use of several string handling functions.

B. Tyers, *GameMaker: Studio 100 Programming Challenges*, DOI 10.1007/978-1-4842-2644-5_74

Guide

You can create a list of letters to check in a single line of code:

```
var alphabet = "abcdefghijklmnopqrstuvwxyz";
```

and then add to an array:

```
for (var i = 1; i < 27; i += 1)
{
    array[i,0] = string_char_at(alphabet, i);//add a letter
    array[i,1] = 0;//set as 0 - will be used for letter count
}
```

You can accept a string and convert it to lowercase:

```
source=get_string("enter a sentence","");//get some data
source=string_lower(source);
```

You can then check each letter and add to an array position:

```
for(var i = 1; i<27; i++)
{
    letter=array[i,0];
    array[i,1]=string_count(letter, source);//get count of letters and add to array
}
```

then draw the output:

```
for (var i = 1; i < 27; i += 1)//loop through array
{
    draw_text(30,i*20,array[i,0]);//draw letter
}
```

CHALLENGE 75

Torpedo Game Remake

Challenge Outline

Player has to direct a torpedo missile to a target, avoiding obstacles. The controls are the following: rotate left and right using arrow keys, or increase speed with the up key.

Level 2

Beginner 2 Hours
Medium 1 Hour
Advanced 30 Minutes

Additional Challenge

Create AI to navigate any path avoiding obstacles.

Points

In Time 20
Additional 20

Notes on Approaching This Challenge

You'll need 3 objects: a player, a wall, and a target. Keypresses can be used to rotate the angle of the player and apply boost; use keyboard_check() for this.

B. Tyers, *GameMaker: Studio 100 Programming Challenges*, DOI 10.1007/978-1-4842-2644-5_75

Guide

You can start an object moving:

```
motion_set(0,2);
```

You can rotate on a keypress, for example:

```
if (keyboard_check(vk_left))  {direction+=2;}
```

You can apply boost:

```
if (keyboard_check(vk_up))  {speed+=1;}
```

You can make the object point in the direction it is moving:

```
image_angle=direction;
```

You can cap its speed:

```
if speed>3 speed=3;
```

You can reduce any boost:

```
if speed>2 speed-=0.1;
```

On collision with a wall, you can restart the game:

```
game_restart();
```

CHALLENGE 76

One Hundred Random Numbers

Challenge Outline

To create a random sequence of the numbers 1 to 100, without repetition. Display the output in 4 columns of 25.

Level 2

Beginner 1 Hour
Medium 20 Minutes
Advanced 10 Minutes

Additional Challenge

Display a single value and position from the ds list. Use the mouse wheel to scroll through the contents.

Points

In Time 20
Additional 20

Notes on Approaching This Challenge

You'll need a suitable data structure to hold the data and one or more types of loop to add and retrieve data. Some basic math will be required to display output in rows and columns.

B. Tyers, *GameMaker: Studio 100 Programming Challenges*, DOI 10.1007/978-1-4842-2644-5_76

Guide

You can create a ds list:

```
list=ds_list_create();
```

You can add to a ds list:

```
ds_list_add(list,value);
```

You can get contents from a ds list, for example, position 5:

```
example=list[| 5];
```

You can create a for loop to loop from 1 to 20 inclusive:

```
for (i = 1; i <= 20; i += 1)
{
        //do something
}
```

You can calculate the remainder of a division (the modulus):

```
answer=21 mod 4;
```

would return 1.

CHALLENGE 77

Coin Flip

Challenge Outline

To simulate the flipping of a coin 100 times. Display whether each flip is heads or tails. Keep track of the results and display results as text.

Level 2

Beginner 1 Hour
Medium 25 Minutes
Advanced 10 Minutes

Additional Challenge

As above, but to display the results as a pie graph that updates after each coin flip.

Points

In Time 20
Additional 20

Notes on Approaching This Challenge

You'll need to create random values and use them to decide whether a head or tail has been flipped. You'll also need extra variables to keep track of how many times each has been thrown. If you want to keep track of all throws made, you could store these in an array.

B. Tyers, *GameMaker: Studio 100 Programming Challenges*, DOI 10.1007/978-1-4842-2644-5_77

Guide

You can use integers to keep track of results, for example:

```
flips=0;
heads=0;
tails=0;
```

You can create an alarm so there is a small pause between flips:

```
alarm[0]=room_speed/2;
```

You can get random values. For example:

```
number=irandom(2);//choose 0, 1 or 2 at random
```

and do something based on that number:

```
if number==1
{
//do something
}
```

You can increment a value:

```
flips++;
```

You can store the value into an array for later use:

```
result[flip]=number;
```

CHALLENGE 78

Predict the Path of an Object

Challenge Outline

To use the motion, friction, and gravity to predict the path of a moving object.

Level 5

Beginner 3 Hours
Medium 1 Hour
Advanced 30 Minutes

Additional Challenge

Make an advanced version that compensates for a wind direction and speed.

Points

In Time 50
Additional 20

Notes on Approaching This Challenge

A script that takes the necessary variables and uses them to store points in a ds_list. This can then be used in either a path or to draw points.

You'll need to perform calculations on the hspeed and vspeed, gravity and gravity direction, and friction.

B. Tyers, *GameMaker: Studio 100 Programming Challenges*, DOI 10.1007/978-1-4842-2644-5_78

Guide

The script code can be found in the resources folder.

This is the drawing code I used:

```
draw_self();//draw the bullet
if !ds_list_empty(points)
{
    size=ds_list_size(points);//get size of grid
    for (var i = 0; i < size; i += 2)//2 steps at a time
    {
        draw_point(points[|i],points[|i+1]);//get value to draw points
    }
}
```

CHALLENGE 79

Dynamic Button

Challenge Outline

To create an object that displays a button with the provided text.
Adapt the button size to fit the text.
Change the button colour depending if the mouse cursor is over the image and again when being pressed.

Level 2

Beginner 40 Minutes
Medium 30 Minutes
Advanced 12 Minutes

Additional Challenge

To create 3 buttons, return which has been clicked.

Points

In Time 20
Additional 20

Notes on Approaching This Challenge

This uses basic drawing commands, but through a script. Use the mouse position to determine whether it is over a drawn button.

B. Tyers, *GameMaker: Studio 100 Programming Challenges*, DOI 10.1007/978-1-4842-2644-5_79

Guide

You can set drawing colour:

```
draw_set_color(c_blue);
```

Image alpha:

```
draw_set_alpha(0.5);
```

You can draw a rectangle:

```
draw_rectangle(x1,y1,x2,y2,false);
```

You can check if the mouse is in certain "rectangle" area:

```
point_in_rectangle(mouse_x,mouse_y,xpos,ypos,xpos2,ypos2);
```

You can set the horizontal alignment drawing for the text:

```
draw_set_halign(fa_center);
```

and the vertical position:

```
draw_set_valign(fa_middle);
```

and draw the text with:

```
draw_text(xx,yy,str);
```

CHALLENGE 80

Sokoban Game Remake

Challenge Outline

To remake the classic Sokoban game where you have to push blocks into holes. The player can move into empty squares or push single blocks into them. Aim is to push all blocks into allocated holes. For level design, see a site such as:

`http://sneezingtiger.com/sokoban/levels.html`

Level 5

Beginner 4 Hours

Medium 3 Hours

Advanced 2 Hours

Additional Challenge

Allow level creation from importing Sokoban levels in text format. There is a standard format for this. Combine this with challenge 13 to retrieve levels from the net. Five have been uploaded to: gamemakerbook.com/sokoban1.txt through to sokoban5.txt

Points

In Time 50

Additional 20

Notes on Approaching This Challenge

You'll need to figure out how to make a movable player, how to push single blocks, and how to detect if a block is over a hole.

B. Tyers, *GameMaker: Studio 100 Programming Challenges*, DOI 10.1007/978-1-4842-2644-5_80

Guide

You can check for an empty square or a block followed by an empty square, for example, to the left:

```
if (keyboard_check(vk_left)) && !((position_meeting(x-18,y,obj_block) && (position_
meeting(x-50,y,obj_block))))
```

You should note that position_meeting is sensitive to the placement of the origin, and the cell size of the room. In this example all objects are 32x32 pixels and the origin is centered for all.

You can then set a value to a variable to initiate movement. For example, left:

```
move_dx = -spd;
```

You could do this in a script, as follows:

```
soko_move(dx, dy)
```

Use the following code at the start of the script:

```
var dx = argument0, nx = x + dx;
var dy = argument1, ny = y + dy;
```

Return false if there's a solid object in the proposed direction:

```
if (place_meeting(nx, ny, obj_wall))
{ return false;}
```

or return true if the space is empty and update the coordinates:

```
if (place_free(nx, ny))
{
    x = nx; y = ny;
    return true;
}
```

CHALLENGE 81

Top Down Football

Challenge Outline

To create a play area with a ball and multiple players. The aim is to kick the ball around. Only the player nearest the ball can move at any one time.

Level 2

Beginner 3 Hours

Medium 1 Hour

Advanced 30 Minutes

Additional Challenge

Create a 2-player game with a goal at each end.

Points

In Time 20

Additional 20

Notes on Approaching This Challenge

You'll need to make the ball bounce off of players and walls. You'll need to find the instance nearest the ball and use the id for movement.

B. Tyers, *GameMaker: Studio 100 Programming Challenges*, DOI 10.1007/978-1-4842-2644-5_81

Guide

To start the ball moving:

```
motion_set(random(359),2);
```

Get the id of the nearest object:

```
inst=instance_nearest(x,y,obj_player);
```

Use this id to make movement:

```
if (keyboard_check(ord('A')))  {inst.x-=5;}
```

On collision you can use:

```
hspeed*=-1;
vspeed*=-1;
```

CHALLENGE 82

Top Down Racing

Challenge Outline

To create a basic track and car that can drive around it. Use left and right steer car and up to accelerate. Cap a maximum speed and apply friction. Set the room as 2000x2000 pixels and the view as 800x800 and to follow player.

Level 2

Beginner 1 Hour
Medium 30 Minutes
Advanced 15 Minutes

Additional Challenge

Create some AI cars for player to race against.

Points

In Time 20
Additional 20

Notes on Approaching This Challenge

Set up keypresses for the movement, and use the built-in variable speed for acceleration and friction. Change the image angle when left and right are pressed and also update direction to this value.

B. Tyers, *GameMaker: Studio 100 Programming Challenges*, DOI 10.1007/978-1-4842-2644-5_82

Guide

You can set the view with:

```
view_enabled[0] = true;
view_visible[0] = true;
view_wview[0]=800;
view_hview[0]=800;
view_object[0]=obj_car;//set object to follow
view_hborder[0] = view_wview[0] / 2;
view_vborder[0] = view_hview[0] / 2;
```

You can rotate the car:

```
if (keyboard_check(vk_left))  {image_angle+=2;}
```

And update the direction to angle:

```
direction=image_angle;
```

You can apply friction:

```
speed=speed*0.98;
```

You can set the speed to 0 if below a threshold, for example, + / - 0.1:

```
if abs(speed)<0.1 speed=0;
```

And make it bounce of a wall:

```
if place_meeting(x,y,obj_wall)
{
    speed*=-1;
}
```

CHALLENGE 83

Convert Numbers (in Digits) to Words

Challenge Outline

The user has to enter a number from 1 to 1000; the program then needs to convert this into words and display the result onscreen. For example 234 would be "Two Hundred and Thirty four."

Level 2

Beginner 1 Hour

Medium 40 Minutes

Advanced 20 Minutes

Additional Challenge

Allow for entry up to 1 billion (1,000,000,000).

Points

In Time 20

Additional 20

Notes on Approaching This Challenge

You can use div and mod to get values from an integer.

B. Tyers, *GameMaker: Studio 100 Programming Challenges*, DOI 10.1007/978-1-4842-2644-5_83

Guide

You can get the user to enter an integer:

```
value=get_integer("Enter number (upto 999)",0);//get string
```

You could get the hundreds value:

```
pos1=value div 100; //hundreds
```

You can make a string for the hundreds:

```
if pos1==2 part1="Two Hundred ";
```

Similarly for the units:

```
pos3=value mod 10; //0 to 9
```

and set a string based on the value:

```
if pos3==6 and pos2!=1 part3="six";
```

You can add strings together:

```
display=pos1 + " "+pos3;
```

CHALLENGE 84

Zelda Style Views

Challenge Outline

To show only part of a room at a time and scroll in the next part of the room when the player leaves the edge.

Level 4

Beginner 2 Hours

Medium 1 Hour

Advanced 45 Minutes

Additional Challenge

Create a sliding sound when view shifts.

Points

In Time 40

Additional 20

Notes on Approaching This Challenge

This focuses on advanced use of views. If you're not familiar with how they and the GML for views work, spend some time looking through the manual.

B. Tyers, *GameMaker: Studio 100 Programming Challenges*, DOI 10.1007/978-1-4842-2644-5_84

Guide

You can set up the initial view and port using code, or alternatively in the room editor:

```
view_enabled[0] = true; view_visible[0] = true; view_wview[0]=240;
view_hview[0]=160; view_xport[0]=0; view_yport[0]=0;
view_wport[0]=240; view_hport[0]=160;
```

You can set up required variables:

```
view_x = view_xview [0]; view_y = view_yview [0];
view_x1 = view_x; view_y1 = view_y;
view_xspeed = 16; view_yspeed = 8;
```

You can update views:

```
if obj_player.x > view_x + view_wview [0] view_x += view_wview [0];
if obj_player.x < view_x view_x -= view_wview [0];
if obj_player.y > view_y + view_hview [0] view_y += view_hview [0];
if obj_player.y < view_y view_y -= view_hview [0];
if view_x1 < view_x view_x1 = min(view_x,view_x1 + view_xspeed);
if view_x1 > view_x view_x1 = max(view_x,view_x1 - view_xspeed);
if view_y1 < view_y view_y1 = min(view_y,view_y1 + view_yspeed);
if view_y1 > view_y view_y1 = max(view_y,view_y1 - view_yspeed);
view_xview [0] = view_x1; view_yview [0] = view_y1;
```

For player movement:

```
dx = (keyboard_check(vk_right) - keyboard_check(vk_left)) * 4;
dy = (keyboard_check(vk_down) - keyboard_check(vk_up)) * 4;
if !place_meeting(x+dx,y,obj_solid) x += dx;
if !place_meeting(x,y+dy,obj_solid) y += dy;
```

CHALLENGE 85

Convert Text File to eBook

Challenge Outline

To convert a text file to an html-based eBook. To include an index page and links on each book page to next and previous pages. Limit each page to around 3000 characters. Use <br> for line beaks. Also use <br> for paragraph breaks (blank lines).
A couple of text ebooks in TXT format are available in the downloads resources, these can be used for testing purposes.

Level 3

Beginner 3 Hours
Medium 1 Hour
Advanced 30 Minutes

Additional Challenge

To combine this with challenge 13 to retrieve a text file from the Internet and convert this into an eBook. A sample file is available at: `http://gamemakerbook.com/dracula.txt`

Points

In Time 30
Additional 20

Notes on Approaching This Challenge

For this you'll need to do some basic file and string handling. You can open the source file and read off parts of it and write to a new file, and repeat this until the whole book is read. You'll also need to learn some basic HTML coding.

B. Tyers, *GameMaker: Studio 100 Programming Challenges*, DOI 10.1007/978-1-4842-2644-5_85

Guide

You can open a TXT file to read from using:

```
source=file_text_open_read("example.txt");
```

You can read a line from the source file:

```
line=file_text_read_string(source);
```

You can skip to the next line:

```
file_text_readln(source);
```

You can open a file to write to:

```
target=file_text_open_write('target.html');
```

You can write to it:

```
file_text_write_string(target,line);
```

You can insert an HTML line break with:

```
file_text_write_string(target,"<br>");
```

You can create an HTML link:

```
string="<BR><BR><A HREF="+chr(34)+ 'filename.html'+chr(34)+">Next Page</A>";
```

After you've completed processing the book, you can view the output by going to HELP>> OPEN PROJECT DATA IN EXPLORER. This will open the data storage area for files created within GameMaker: Studio's sandboxed area.

CHALLENGE 86

Planets Database (INI)

Challenge Outline

To extract data from the provided INI file (in resources) and display onscreen. Allow left and right arrows to change planet. The INI file has separate sections for each planet, and a key for each of data elements. All are in string format.

Level 3

Beginner 2 Hours

Medium 1 Hour

Advanced 30 Minutes

Additional Challenge

Allow the user to enter up to 3 more data sets for each planet, and up to 4 more planets. Update the INI file to store this new data.

Points

In Time 30

Additional 20

Notes on Approaching This Challenge

GameMaker has a comprehensive assortment of INI-related functions. For this challenge you'll need to open an INI file and read the data to a suitable data structure and draw on-screen.

B. Tyers, *GameMaker: Studio 100 Programming Challenges*, DOI 10.1007/978-1-4842-2644-5_86

Guide

The basic method for INI file use is, first open file:

```
ini_open("planets.ini")
value=ini_read_string("section","key","default");
```

You can store a value in an array, for example:

```
data[0,0]=value;
```

Reading straight from an open ini file:

```
for (i = 0; i < planets; i += 1)//loop through no of planets
{
   if i=0 planet="mercury"//set section name
   if i=1 planet="venus"
   if i=2 planet="earth"
   data[i,0]=ini_read_string(planet,"name","");//read from section and key
   data[i,1]=ini_read_string(planet,"distance_to_sun","");
   data[i,2]=ini_read_string(planet,"year_length","");
   data[i,3]=ini_read_string(planet,"mass","");
   data[i,4]=ini_read_string(planet,"escape_velocity","");
   data[i,5]=ini_read_string(planet,"max_temp","");
   data[i,6]=ini_read_string(planet,"min_temp","");
}
```

You can change a value on a keypress, for example:

```
if (keyboard_check_released(vk_left))  {current-=1;}
```

and keep it in a range:

```
if current==-1 current=planets-1;
```

CHALLENGE 87

How Much Flour

Challenge Outline

You work at a bakery. You use flour to make bread. Flour comes in bags of 7, 3, and 1KG. The baker tells you how many kg of flour he needs. Calculate how many of each bag size are needed, using the minimum number of bags possible.

Level 2

Beginner 1 Hour
Medium 25 Minutes
Advanced 8 Minutes

Additional Challenge

Create an onscreen slider that allows you to input between 1 and 1000kg. Update how many bags of each in real time.

Points

In Time 20
Additional 20

Notes on Approaching This Challenge

This is mainly a mathematical challenge. An operator (`div`) will come in handy here. There are a few ways to approach this; you can use the `mod` operator if you wish.

B. Tyers, *GameMaker: Studio 100 Programming Challenges*, DOI 10.1007/978-1-4842-2644-5_87

Guide

div can be used to find out how many times a number can fully go into another, for example:

```
value=20 div 7;
```

would set value as 2.
Mod can be used to return the remainder of a division. For example

```
value=20 mod 7;
```

would set value as 6.

CHALLENGE 88

Rotating Mini Map

Challenge Outline

To draw a mini map of objects in the player's vicinity that rotates based on the direction to the mouse cursor.

Level 5

Beginner 3 Hours

Medium 1 Hour

Advanced 30 Minutes

Additional Challenge

Add 3 more objects and get them drawn on the mini map.

Points

In Time 50

Additional 20

Notes on Approaching This Challenge

This combines math and basic drawing functions.

This challenge requires some knowledge of linear interpolation.

A script is ideal for this.

B. Tyers, *GameMaker: Studio 100 Programming Challenges*, DOI 10.1007/978-1-4842-2644-5_88

Guide

You can set up an instance of an object to move toward the mouse's position if more than 2 pixels away:

```
if distance_to_point(mouse_x,mouse_y)>2
{
    dir=point_direction(x,y,mouse_x,mouse_y);//get direction to mouse
    motion_set(dir,4);//mouse to mouse
}
else speed=0;
```

Here is some code that will be useful:
Draw a line between two points:

```
draw_line(obj_center.x, obj_center.y, mouse_x, mouse_y);
```

You can perform calculations based on the variable of another instance:

```
with (obj_unit)
{
        //do somthing
}
```

You can push a transformation:

```
d3d_transform_stack_push();
```

and rotate a transformation:

```
d3d_transform_add_rotation_z(angle);
```

CHALLENGE 89

Selectable Troops

Challenge Outline

Create a system that allows you to draw a rectangle by clicking and holding the mouse button and selecting any troops within that area. Highlight selected troops.

Level 4

Beginner 3 Hours

Medium 1 Hour

Advanced 30 Minutes

Additional Challenge

Allow the right button to move troops, in the same formation to where mouse is clicked, based on average position of all troops.

Points

In Time 40

Additional 20

Notes on Approaching This Challenge

You'll need to detect a mouse button being pressed and remember its position; also draw a rectangle to where the mouse button is being held.

B. Tyers, *GameMaker: Studio 100 Programming Challenges*, DOI 10.1007/978-1-4842-2644-5_89

Guide

You can get and store mouse coordinates (use on initial mouse press):

```
select_x1 = mouse_x;
select_y1 = mouse_y;
```

and while mouse is pressed down:

```
select_x2 = mouse_x;
select_y2 = mouse_y;
```

You can check for instances within a rectangle, for example:

```
with (obj_unit)
{
if (!collision_rectangle(x1, y1, x2, y2, id, false, false)) {//do something}
}
```

In the code above x1 and y1 are the point when mouse was initially pressed and x2 and y2 are the current mouse's position.

You can store the id of an object:

```
value = id;
```

Then add the value to an array or ds structure:

```
array[0]=value;
```

You can draw a rectangle:

```
draw_rectangle(x1,y1,x2,y2,true);
```

You can also draw a rectangle using the id of an object for the x and y positions:

```
u = array[0];
draw_rectangle(u.x,u.y,u.x+50,u.y+50, true);
```

CHALLENGE 90

Pipes

Challenge Outline

To allow the user to place pipes within a room and connect up with any pipes next to the newly placed pipe.
Sprites for this are in the resources pack.

Level 5

Beginner 3 Hours
Medium 1 Hour
Advanced 30 Minutes

Additional Challenge

Create a tap and a drain. The player has to connect them up using as few pipes as possible, avoiding any obstacles you place in the way.

Points

In Time 50
Additional 20

Notes on Approaching This Challenge

First check the clicked place is collision free. Place a pipe object in this position, and then check above, below and left, and right to find out which pipe fitting (sprite) you need. This could be done one by one using code, or a user-created event (see guide).

B. Tyers, *GameMaker: Studio 100 Programming Challenges*, DOI 10.1007/978-1-4842-2644-5_90

Guide

You can check if a position is free, create a pipe, and update:

```
if !position_meeting(mouse_x, mouse_y, obj_pipe)
{
    cx = floor(mouse_x / 32) * 32
    cy = floor(mouse_y / 32) * 32
    instance_create(cx, cy, obj_pipe)
    instance_create(cx, cy, obj_updater)
}
```

You can create a user-defined event, for example, User Defined 0:

```
// event_user(0)
//some code
```

Using binary representation, you can use some cool math to update a cell based on its neigbors:

```
var t, b, l, r, d, j;
j = object_index;
d = 32;
t = place_meeting(x, y - d, j);
b = place_meeting(x, y + d, j);
r = place_meeting(x + d, y, j);
l = place_meeting(x - d, y, j);
image_index = l + r * 2 + t * 4 + b * 8;
```

which would set image_index to a value between 0 and 15. The images for this are in the resources.

CHALLENGE 91

Arcade Style Horse Race Game

Challenge Outline

To re-create the classic coin op game where horses move at random speeds from left to right.
Create 4 horses and have them race each other.
Sprites for the horses are in the resource pack.

Level 2

Beginner 1 Hour
Medium 25 Minutes
Advanced 15 Minutes

Additional Challenge

Determine and display the race times of each horse.

Points

In Time 20
Additional 20

Notes on Approaching This Challenge

An ideal way to do this is have a button that spawns all 4 horses. When it's created, set it to move right at a random speed and have a random alarm. On the alarm, change the horse's speed and reset the alarm. Keep the horse at a minimum speed.

B. Tyers, *GameMaker: Studio 100 Programming Challenges*, DOI 10.1007/978-1-4842-2644-5_91

Guide

You can create an instance of an object, for example:

```
instance_create(20,100,obj_horse_1);
```

You can set a horse moving right:

```
motion_set(0,irandom_range(1,3));
```

and set an alarm:

```
alarm[0]=irandom(3*room_speed);
```

You can change the speed with:

```
motion_add(0,irandom_range(-2,2));
```

and keep at a minimum speed of 1:

```
if hspeed<1 hspeed=1;
```

You can keep the image animation proportional to the move speed with:

```
image_speed=hspeed/4;
```

Finally on collision with a finish line instance, declare the winner:

```
show_message("Horse 1 Wins");
room_restart();
```

CHALLENGE 92

Road Builder

Challenge Outline

To allow the player to add more road instances to an existing road.

Level 4

Beginner 2 Hours

Medium 1 Hour

Advanced 30 Minutes

Additional Challenge

Allow right-click to place tree instances that roads cannot be built on.

Points

In Time 40

Additional 20

Notes on Approaching This Challenge

You'll have to check if the mouse button is pressed on an existing road section and set a flag. Then as the mouse is being dragged, check it connects to an existing road section using this flag.

B. Tyers, *GameMaker: Studio 100 Programming Challenges*, DOI 10.1007/978-1-4842-2644-5_92

Guide

You can set the initial flag to:

```
can_build = false;
```

You can then check if you're next to an existing road, for example, there is one above:

```
can_build=place_meeting(cursor_x - 1, cursor_y, road);
```

Then create a road:

```
instance_create(cursor_x, cursor_y, obj_road);
```

CHALLENGE 93

Chess Board Representation

Challenge Outline

To draw a chess board and pieces. Allow pieces to be moved by clicking and dragging (no AI). Allow the left mouse button to pick up a piece and the right button to place it.

Level 2

Beginner 3 Hours
Medium 1 Hour
Advanced 30 Minutes

Additional Challenge

Only allow for valid moves.

Points

In Time 20
Additional 20

Notes on Approaching This Challenge

The board can be drawn using loops and rectangles. Make a single parent object, then assign each piece type as a child of it. On a left mouse click, get the unique id of the instance and use that until the piece has been placed.

B. Tyers, *GameMaker: Studio 100 Programming Challenges*, DOI 10.1007/978-1-4842-2644-5_93

Guide

Here's one method of drawing a board, but lots more variations exist:

```
for (var xx = 0; xx < 8; xx += 1)
{ for (var yy = 0; yy < 8; yy += 1)
 {colour=(xx+yy) mod 2;
        if colour=1 draw_set_colour(c_white); else draw_set_colour(c_black);
        draw_rectangle(xx*64, yy*64, (xx+1)*64, (yy+1)*64, false); } }
```

You can set a selected flag:

```
selected=false;
```

then use this to check you can pick up an object:

```
if position_meeting(mouse_x,mouse_y,id) && mouse_check_button_pressed(mb_left) && !selected
{ xoffset=x-mouse_x; yoffset=y-mouse_y; selected=true;}
else
{ xoffset=0; yoffset=0;}
```

Keep the object the same distance from mouse click (offset):

```
if selected/run this every step
{   x=mouse_x+xoffset;//move to mouse x, applying offset
    y=mouse_y+yoffset;//move to mouse y, applying offset
    move_snap(32,32); }
```

Drop the object and unselect on right mouse button:

```
if selected && mouse_check_button_pressed(mb_right)//drop the piece
{selected=false;}
```

CHALLENGE 94

1945 Game Remake

Challenge Outline

To create the classic style of game play for 1945. A player at the bottom of the room controls a ship and fires bullets at enemy planes coming from the top. Some enemies fire bullets back. If a player shoots down an enemy, that get points. If they are hit by an enemy bullet, they lose health.

Level 2

Beginner 2 Hours

Medium 1 Hour

Advanced 40 Minutes

Additional Challenge

Create an additional enemy that fires toward the player's position every 3 seconds.

Points

In Time 20

Additional 20

Notes on Approaching This Challenge

For this task you'll need basic movement and collision code, with some variable coding for lives and score.

B. Tyers, *GameMaker: Studio 100 Programming Challenges*, DOI 10.1007/978-1-4842-2644-5_94

Guide

For simple movement, you can use, for example:

```
if (keyboard_check(vk_left))  {x-=5;}
```

For detecting a letter press:

```
if (keyboard_check_presseed(ord('Z')))
{
        //do something
}
```

To create an instance:

```
instance_create(x,y,obj_player_bullet);
```

To set an instance moving, for example down at a speed of 5:

```
motion_set(270, 5);
```

To increase score:

```
score+=10;
```

To reduce health:

```
health-=1;
```

To destroy another object in collision event:

```
with (other) instance_destroy();
```

CHALLENGE 95

Create a Virtual ATM (Bank Teller)

Challenge Outline

Create a virtual ATM (bank teller) that keeps a record of 10 card numbers, PIN codes, and bank balances.
Allow user to enter card number and PIN and withdraw cash if available.
Update bank balance accordingly.

Level 3

Beginner 2 Hours
Medium 1 Hour
Advanced 25 Minutes

Additional Challenge

Create a numerical keypad for users to enter data.
Display withdrawn cash as images on screen.
ATM to keep track of notes left in machine.

Points

In Time 30
Additional 20

Notes on Approaching This Challenge

You'll need some kind of data structure to hold account number, PIN, and balance. You'll need to compare data entered by the user to the data in the data structure.

B. Tyers, *GameMaker: Studio 100 Programming Challenges*, DOI 10.1007/978-1-4842-2644-5_95

Guide

You can enter data to an array:

```
account[0,0]="123456";//account no
account[0,1]="1234";//pin
account[0,2]=200;//balance
```

You can get string from user:

```
example_string=get_string("account no","");
```

You can get an integer from user:

```
example_integer=get_integer("How Much To Withdrawal",0);
```

You can take a value off an array entry:

```
account[0,2]-=value;
```

You can compare values (less or equal to):

```
if value1<=value2
{
        //do something
}
```

CHALLENGE 96

Moon Lander Game Remake

Challenge Outline

To create a steerable spaceship that can move left and right by applying a force in the direction, and by applying an upward force. Also simulate some gravity. The aim is to land on a platform at the bottom of room.

Level 1

Beginner 1 Hour

Medium 20 Minutes

Advanced 10 Minutes

Additional Challenge

Create some moving asteroids that the player needs to avoid.

Points

In Time 10

Additional 20

Notes on Approaching This Challenge

You'll need to detect keypresses and change vspeed and hspeed accordingly. You'll need to increase vspeed constantly to give a gravity type effect.

B. Tyers, *GameMaker: Studio 100 Programming Challenges*, DOI 10.1007/978-1-4842-2644-5_96

Guide

You can detect a keypress, for example:

```
if (keyboard_check(vk_left))
{
        //do somthing
}
```

You can use hspeed to add movement, for example, to the right:

```
hspeed+=0.16;
```

You can simulate friction:

```
hspeed*=0.99;
```

You can stop hspeed if below a certain value:

```
if abs(hspeed)<0.05 hspeed=0;
```

You can make the ship move up:

```
vspeed-=0.16;
```

or apply a gravity effect:

```
vspeed+=0.02;
```

You can use abs to detect within a range, for example, -1 and 1:

```
if abs(vspeed)<1
{
        //do something
}
```

CHALLENGE 97

Pixelate an Image

Challenge Outline

To get colour values from points in a picture and use these values to re-draw the values to create a pixelated effect.

Level 5

Beginner 3 Hours
Medium 1 Hour
Advanced 30 Minutes

Additional Challenge

Allow user to set pixelation size and output to as an image file, with screen_sav_part() or surface_save().

Points

In Time 50
Additional 20

Notes on Approaching This Challenge

You'll need to get the colour from various points in the image and store the values in a suitable data structure. Nested loops would great for getting values and writing to the data structure. You'll then need to use this data to redraw the image.

B. Tyers, *GameMaker: Studio 100 Programming Challenges*, DOI 10.1007/978-1-4842-2644-5_97

Guide

You can get the colour value from a position:

```
col=draw_getpixel(x_pos,y_pos);
```

You can add data to an array. For example:

```
global.data[0,0]=col;
```

You can set the drawing colour:

```
draw_set_colour(value);
```

You can draw a solid rectangle:

```
draw_rectangle(x_pos1,y_pos1,x_pos2,y_pos2,false);
```

You create a nested loop:

```
for (i = 0; i < 10; i += 1)
{
    for (j = 0; j  < 10; j += 1)
        {
        //do something
        }
}
```

You can get the width / height of a sprite, for example:

```
value=sprite_get_width(spr_example);
```

CHALLENGE 98

Miner

Challenge Outline

To create a top down mining system where the player can destroy and build blocks. Allow left-click to destroy a block and right-click to build one.
Sprites for this are available in the resources.

Level 3

Beginner 3 Hours
Medium 1 Hour
Advanced 30 Minutes

Additional Challenge

Create 6 types of blocks. Keep track of how many of each block have been mined.

Points

In Time 30
Additional 20

Notes on Approaching This Challenge

Allow movement through arrow keys. Create a parent object for blocks (to allow adding more types easily). Use the parent object to draw over child to indicate mining progress of the object. On right-click check position is free and create a block if it is, snapped to 32x32.

B. Tyers, *GameMaker: Studio 100 Programming Challenges*, DOI 10.1007/978-1-4842-2644-5_98

Guide

Simple movement to check for empty space in direction:

```
dx = (keyboard_check(vk_right) - keyboard_check(vk_left)) * 4;
dy = (keyboard_check(vk_down) - keyboard_check(vk_up)) * 4;
if place_free(x + dx, y + dy)//check if direction clear
{ x += dx; y += dy; }
```

To create new block:

```
if mouse_check_button_pressed(mb_right) && !position_meeting(mouse_x, mouse_y, obj_block)
&& !position_meeting(mouse_x, mouse_y, obj_hero)
{ instance_create(32 * (mouse_x div 32), 32 * (mouse_y div 32), obj_stone); }
```

For mining:

```
if mouse_check_button(mb_left) && position_meeting(mouse_x,mouse_y,id)
{
    //do something, for example damage a block by reducing local hp
}
```

Undo mining if left before finished:

```
if mouse_check_button_released(mb_left)
{ durc = 0; }
```

To draw current damage:

```
draw_sprite(spr_damage, floor(10 * durc), x, y);
```

CHALLENGE 99

Follow Player (Ghost)

Challenge Outline

Create a movable player object, and an enemy that moves toward the player. Place some instances of an obstacle that the player and enemy should avoid.

Level 2

Beginner 3 Hours
Medium 1 Hour
Advanced 30 Minutes

Additional Challenge

Make the ghost move faster if it gets too far behind.

Points

In Time 20
Additional 20

Notes on Approaching This Challenge

You'll need to add points to a path and have the ghost follow this path. You'll need some collision system to prevent the player moving through an obstacle.

B. Tyers, *GameMaker: Studio 100 Programming Challenges*, DOI 10.1007/978-1-4842-2644-5_99

Guide

You can move using the following, for example, to the left if there is no instance of obj_obstacle in that direction:

```
if (keyboard_check(vk_left))  && !place_meeting(x-4,y,obj_obstacle)
{
    x-=4;
}
```

You can create a grid that will be used for path finding:

```
size = 16;
grid = mp_grid_create(0,0,ceil(room_width/size),ceil(room_height/size),size,size);
```

You can add cells that the path cannot go through:

```
mp_grid_add_instances(grid,obj_obstacle,1);
```

You can set up a path:

```
path=path_add();
```

The use the grid to find a path between 2 points:

```
mp_grid_path(grid,path,x,y,obj_player.x,obj_player.y,1);
```

You can start a path:

```
path_start(path,2,path_action_stop,true);
```

You can check for a path end using End Path Event or code:

```
if path_position==1
```

CHALLENGE 100

Multiplication Table

Challenge Outline

To draw onscreen a standard 12x12 multiplication table.

Level 1

Beginner 1 Hour
Medium 20 Minutes
Advanced 8 Minutes

Additional Challenge

To include a grid and to change background colour of any cell upon mouseover.

Points

In Time 10
Additional 20

Notes on Approaching This Challenge

For this you will need to use nested loops and text drawing.

B. Tyers, *GameMaker: Studio 100 Programming Challenges*, DOI 10.1007/978-1-4842-2644-5_100

Guide

You can draw a variable on the screen using:

```
draw_text(x,y,value);
```

You can do multiplication:

```
value=a*b;
```

You can do a nested loop:

```
for (var i = 1; i < 5; i += 1)
for (var j = 1; j < 5; j += 1)
{
    //do something
}
```

APPENDIX A

Points Chart

Challenge 1	Challenge 2	Challenge 3	Challenge 4	Challenge 5
Available: 40 Your Score:	Available: 30 Your Score:	Available: 30 Your Score:	Available: 40 Your Score:	Available: 40 Your Score:

Total Available For 1 To 5: 180

135-180	>>	**Maestro**
110-135	>>	**Game Master**
90-110	>>	**Doing OK**
70-90	>>	**Could Do Better**
0-70	>>	**Need to Try Harder**

Challenge 6	Challenge 7	Challenge 8	Challenge 9	Challenge 10
Available: 40 Your Score:	Available: 40 Your Score:	Available: 30 Your Score:	Available: 40 Your Score:	Available: 40 Your Score:

Total Available For 6 To 10: 190

150-190	>>	**Maestro**
120-150	>>	**Game Master**
100-120	>>	**Doing OK**
80-100	>>	**Could Do Better**
0-80	>>	**Need to Try Harder**

Challenge 11	Challenge 12	Challenge 13	Challenge 14	Challenge 15
Available: 30 Your Score:	Available: 30 Your Score:	Available: 40 Your Score:	Available: 50 Your Score:	Available: 50 Your Score:

Total Available For 1 To 15: 200

160-200	>>	**Maestro**
130-160	>>	**Game Master**
100-130	>>	**Doing OK**
80-100	>>	**Could Do Better**
0-80	>>	**Need to Try Harder**

B. Tyers, *GameMaker: Studio 100 Programming Challenges*, DOI 10.1007/978-1-4842-2644-5

Challenge 16	Challenge 17	Challenge 18	Challenge 19	Challenge 20
Available: 30 Your Score:	Available: 30 Your Score:	Available: 70 Your Score:	Available: 60 Your Score:	Available: 30 Your Score:

Total Available For 16 To 20: 220

170-220	>>	**Maestro**
140-170	>>	**Game Master**
110-140	>>	**Doing OK**
90-110	>>	**Could Do Better**
0-90	>>	**Need to Try Harder**

Challenge 21	Challenge 22	Challenge 23	Challenge 24	Challenge 25
Available: 50 Your Score:	Available: 30 Your Score:	Available: 40 Your Score:	Available: 50 Your Score:	Available: 40 Your Score:

Total Available For 21 To 25: 210

170-210	>>	**Maestro**
135-170	>>	**Game Master**
110-135	>>	**Doing OK**
85-110	>>	**Could Do Better**
0-85	>>	**Need to Try Harder**

Challenge 26	Challenge 27	Challenge 28	Challenge 29	Challenge 30
Available: 50 Your Score:	Available: 40 Your Score:	Available: 50 Your Score:	Available: 30 Your Score:	Available: 40 Your Score:

Total Available For 26 To 30: 210

170-210	>>	**Maestro**
135-170	>>	**Game Master**
110-135	>>	**Doing OK**
85-110	>>	**Could Do Better**
0-85	>>	**Need to Try Harder**

Challenge 31	Challenge 32	Challenge 33	Challenge 34	Challenge 35
Available: 30 Your Score:	Available: 60 Your Score:	Available: 60 Your Score:	Available: 50 Your Score:	Available: 40 Your Score:

Total Available For 31 To 35: 240

190-240	>>	**Maestro**
155-190	>>	**Game Master**
120-155	>>	**Doing OK**
100-120	>>	**Could Do Better**
0-100	>>	**Need to Try Harder**

Challenge 36	Challenge 37	Challenge 38	Challenge 39	Challenge 40
Available: 40 Your Score:	Available: 30 Your Score:	Available: 60 Your Score:	Available: 40 Your Score:	Available: 40 Your Score:

Total Available For 36 To 40: 210

170-210	>>	**Maestro**
135-170	>>	**Game Master**
110-135	>>	**Doing OK**
85-110	>>	**Could Do Better**
0-85	>>	**Need to Try Harder**

Challenge 41	Challenge 42	Challenge 43	Challenge 44	Challenge 45
Available: 50 Your Score:	Available: 30 Your Score:	Available: 30 Your Score:	Available: 70 Your Score:	Available: 30 Your Score:

Total Available For 41 To 45: 210

170-210	>>	**Maestro**
135-170	>>	**Game Master**
110-135	>>	**Doing OK**
85-110	>>	**Could Do Better**
0-85	>>	**Need to Try Harder**

Challenge 46	Challenge 47	Challenge 48	Challenge 49	Challenge 50
Available: 30 Your Score:	Available: 50 Your Score:	Available: 40 Your Score:	Available: 30 Your Score:	Available: 30 Your Score:

Total Available For 46 To 50: 180

135-180	>>	**Maestro**
110-135	>>	**Game Master**
90-110	>>	**Doing OK**
70-90	>>	**Could Do Better**
0-70	>>	**Need to Try Harder**

Challenge 51	Challenge 52	Challenge 53	Challenge 54	Challenge 55
Available: 40 Your Score:	Available: 30 Your Score:	Available: 60 Your Score:	Available: 60 Your Score:	Available: 50 Your Score:

Total Available For 51 To 55: 240

190-240	>>	**Maestro**
150-190	>>	**Game Master**
120-150	>>	**Doing OK**
100-120	>>	**Could Do Better**
0-100	>>	**Need to Try Harder**

Challenge 56	Challenge 57	Challenge 58	Challenge 59	Challenge 60
Available: 70 Your Score:	Available: 30 Your Score:	Available: 30 Your Score:	Available: 40 Your Score:	Available: 30 Your Score:

Total Available For 56 To 60: 200

160-200	>>	**Maestro**
130-160	>>	**Game Master**
100-130	>>	**Doing OK**
80-100	>>	**Could Do Better**
0-100	>>	**Need to Try Harder**

Challenge 61	Challenge 62	Challenge 63	Challenge 64	Challenge 65
Available: 30 Your Score:	Available: 30 Your Score:	Available: 60 Your Score:	Available: 50 Your Score:	Available: 40 Your Score:

Total Available For 61 To 65: 210

170-210	>>	**Maestro**
135-170	>>	**Game Master**
110-135	>>	**Doing OK**
85-110	>>	**Could Do Better**
0-85	>>	**Need to Try Harder**

Challenge 66	Challenge 67	Challenge 68	Challenge 69	Challenge 70
Available: 30 Your Score:	Available: 70 Your Score:	Available: 30 Your Score:	Available: 40 Your Score:	Available: 30 Your Score:

Total Available For 66 To 70: 200

160-200	>>	**Maestro**
130-160	>>	**Game Master**
100-130	>>	**Doing OK**
80-100	>>	**Could Do Better**
0-100	>>	**Need to Try Harder**

Challenge 71	Challenge 72	Challenge 73	Challenge 74	Challenge 75
Available: 30 Your Score:	Available: 30 Your Score:	Available: 40 Your Score:	Available: 50 Your Score:	Available: 40 Your Score:

Total Available For 71 To 75: 190

150-190	>>	**Maestro**
120-150	>>	**Game Master**
100-120	>>	**Doing OK**
75-100	>>	**Could Do Better**
0-75	>>	**Need to Try Harder**

Challenge 76	Challenge 77	Challenge 78	Challenge 79	Challenge 80
Available: 40 Your Score:	Available: 40 Your Score:	Available: 70 Your Score:	Available: 40 Your Score:	Available: 70 Your Score:

Total Available For 76 To 80: 260

200-260	>>	**Maestro**
170-200	>>	**Game Master**
130-170	>>	**Doing OK**
110-130	>>	**Could Do Better**
0-110	>>	**Need to Try Harder**

Challenge 81	Challenge 82	Challenge 83	Challenge 84	Challenge 85
Available: 40 Your Score:	Available: 40 Your Score:	Available: 40 Your Score:	Available: 60 Your Score:	Available: 50 Your Score:

Total Available For 81 To 85: 230

190-230	>>	**Maestro**
150-190	>>	**Game Master**
120-150	>>	**Doing OK**
90-120	>>	**Could Do Better**
0-90	>>	**Need to Try Harder**

Challenge 86	Challenge 87	Challenge 88	Challenge 89	Challenge 90
Available: 50 Your Score:	Available: 40 Your Score:	Available: 70 Your Score:	Available: 60 Your Score:	Available: 70 Your Score:

Total Available For 86 To 90: 290

230-290	>>	**Maestro**
190-230	>>	**Game Master**
150-190	>>	**Doing OK**
120-150	>>	**Could Do Better**
0-120	>>	**Need to Try Harder**

Challenge 91	Challenge 92	Challenge 93	Challenge 94	Challenge 95
Available: 40 Your Score:	Available: 60 Your Score:	Available: 40 Your Score:	Available: 40 Your Score:	Available: 50 Your Score:

Total Available For 91 To 95: 230

190-230	>>	**Maestro**
150-190	>>	**Game Master**
120-150	>>	**Doing OK**
90-120	>>	**Could Do Better**
0-90	>>	**Need to Try Harder**

Challenge 96	Challenge 97	Challenge 98	Challenge 99	Challenge 100
Available: 30 Your Score:	Available: 70 Your Score:	Available: 50 Your Score:	Available: 40 Your Score:	Available: 30 Your Score:

Total Available For 96 To 100: 220

175-220	>>	**Maestro**
140-175	>>	**Game Master**
110-140	>>	**Doing OK**
90-110	>>	**Could Do Better**
0-90	>>	**Need to Try Harder**

Total For All 100 Challenges: 4,300

3,500-4,500	>>	**Maestro**
2,750-3,500	>>	**Game Master**
2,200-2,750	>>	**Doing OK**
1,750-2,200	>>	**Could Do Better**
1,400-1,750	>>	**Need to Try Harder**

Index

B. Tyers, *GameMaker: Studio 100 Programming Challenges*, DOI 10.1007/978-1-4842-2644-5

M

N

O

P, Q

R

S

T

U

V

W

X, Y

Z

Printed in the United States
By Bookmasters